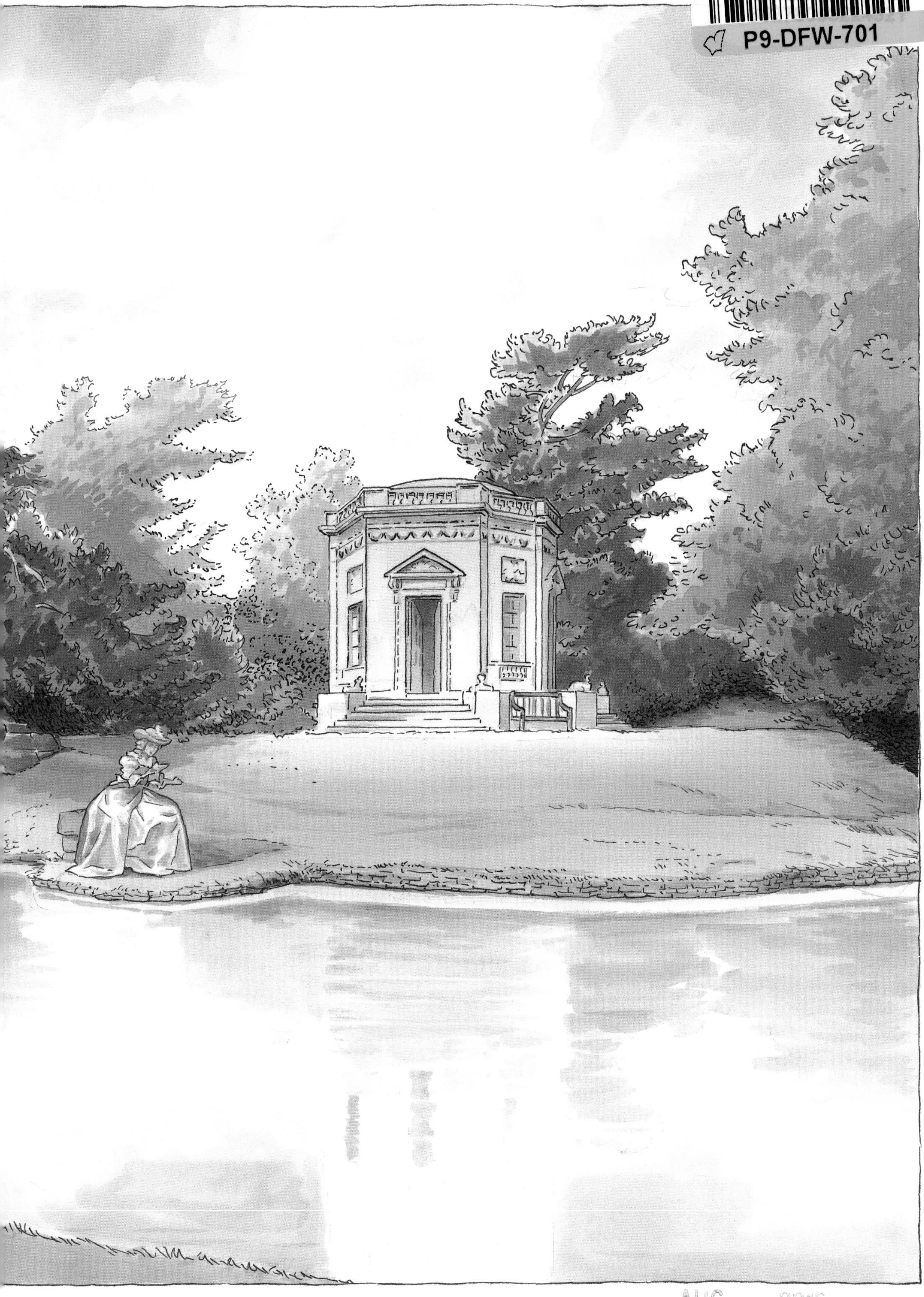

MARIE ANTOINETTE

also available by Annie Goetzinger:

Girl in Dior, quarterbound embossed hardcover

Annie Goetzinger
Girl in
Dior

Other NBM graphic novels to discover:

Beauty (hardcover, e-book)
"Satiric, flamboyant fairy tale."
-Library Journal

Beauty

Miss Don't Touch Me (hardcover, e-book)
"Beautifully illustrated with Kerascoët's magical, dreamy, richly coloured art." **-Publishers Weekly Starred review**

Hubert & Kerascoet
MISS DON'T TOUCH ME
The Complete Story

Borden Tragedy (paperback, e-book)
"This is the primer on a perpetually fascinating, unsolved mystery." **-Booklist**

The Borden Tragedy
Rick Geary

Bubbles & Gondola (hardcover, e-book)
"A certain magic is demonstrated when an artist, unfettered by perceptions of comics being for kids, uses the full paint box of tools available to him."
-Publishers Weekly starred review

Renaud Dillies
Bubbles
&
Gondola

See previews, get exclusives and order from:
NBMPUB.COM

we have over 200 titles available
Catalog upon request
NBM
160 Broadway, Suite 700, East Wing
New York, NY 10038

This graphic novel is also available as an e-book

ISBN 9781681120294
Initially published in French as *Marie Antoinette, La Reine Fantome*

LC control number 2016939080
Translation by Peter Russella
Lettering by Ortho
Printed in Korea
1st printing August 2016

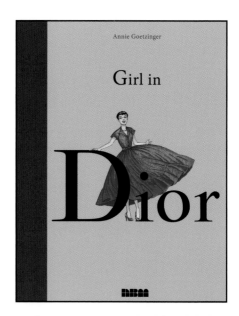

MARIE ANTOINETTE

Phantom Queen

writers: Rodolphe & Annie Goetzinger
art and color: Annie Goetzinger

nbm GRAPHIC NOVELS
Nantier · Beall · Minoustchine
NEW YORK

Annie Goetzinger and I have something in common: a love of ghosts! Not the ones who howl or rattle their chains or spook people, but the sweet, sad shadows who cannot manage to find peace.

Wandering along the banks of the Seine a few years ago, I discovered a small book dedicated to the "ghost" of the Trianon. I took great joy in reading it and of course passed it along to Annie. The work recounted a strange day in Versailles in August of 1901. Two English women, Miss Moberly and Miss Jourdain, came across what seemed to be the ghost of Queen Marie Antoinette in the Garden of the Petit Trianon! This meeting went on to dramatically change the course of these two women's lives. It inspired incessant historical studies and brought them to pen scores of versions of their adventure all in the hopes of refuting their countless critics. Theirs is a story of a very bizarre event that can all too easily be brushed off with a snigger and a simple wave of the hand. What did these women really see? What happened to them on August 10, 1901? We do not know. The least we can say is that something happened…

Since our shared reading of the very first book (prefaced by Jean Cocteau), we have been playing around with the possibility of one day paying homage to this unique adventure, developing the tale of their encounter via a graphic novel…

When we finally got around to putting pen to paper, we found that the adventures of the Two Englishwomen made for a very thin tale indeed…

Gladly leaving them behind, our telling of the story tamps down their emotional experience while providing a context for the royal phantom, along with new plot and explanation…

May the ghost queen one day forgive us!

…And of course Misses Moberly and Jourdain, too!

Rodolphe

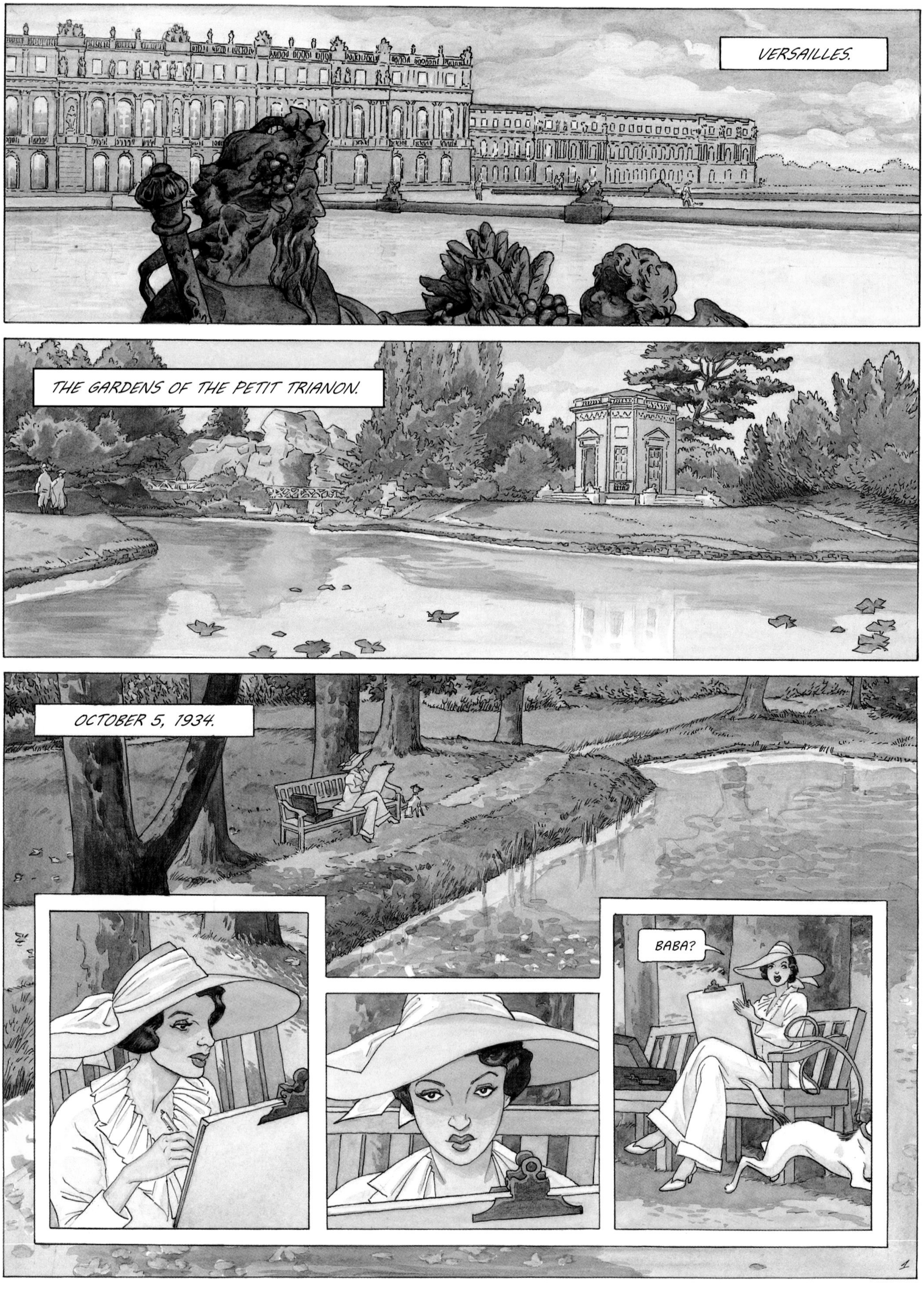
VERSAILLES.
THE GARDENS OF THE PETIT TRIANON.
OCTOBER 5, 1934.
BABA?
1

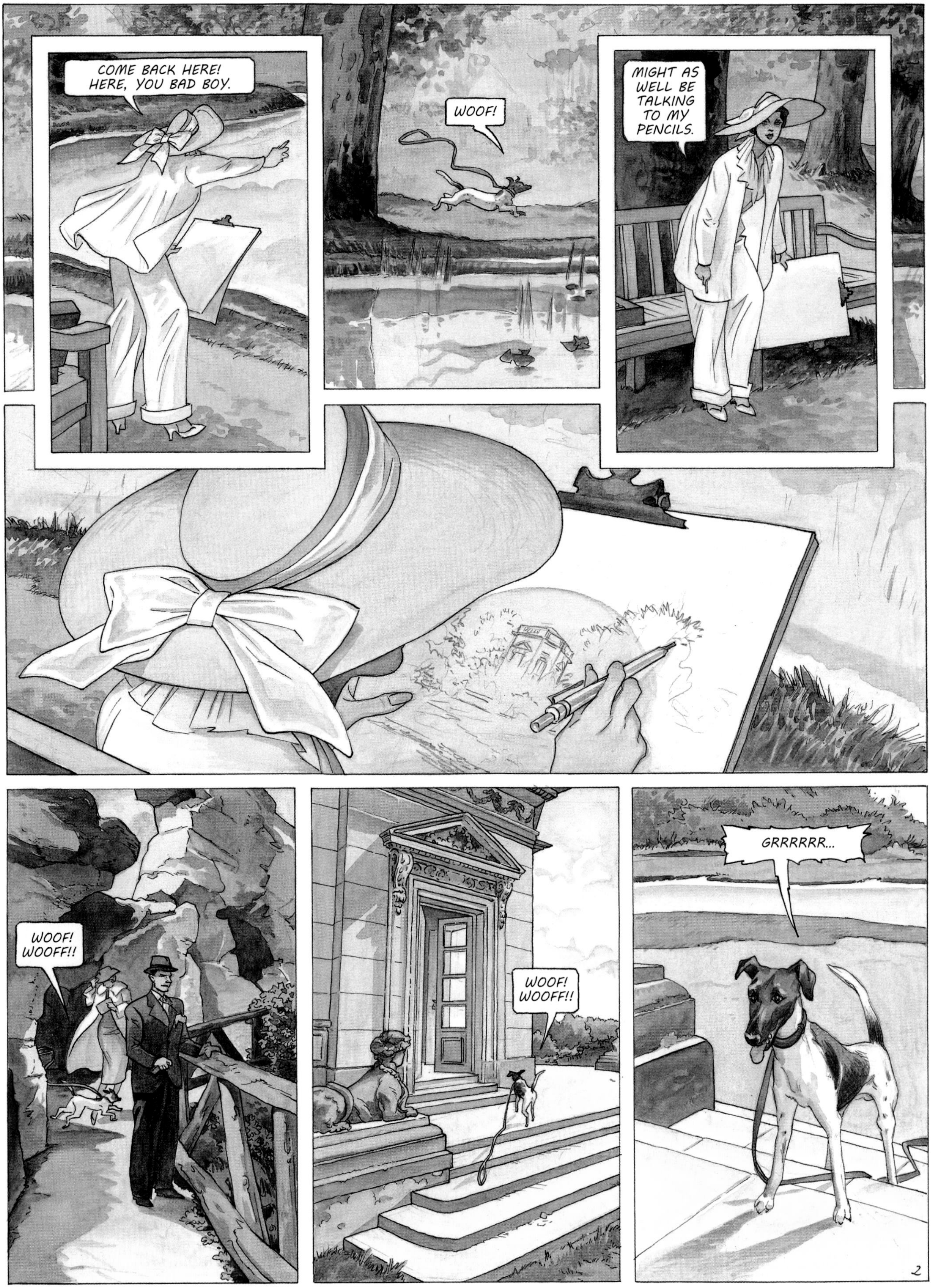
COME BACK HERE! HERE, YOU BAD BOY.
WOOF!
MIGHT AS WELL BE TALKING TO MY PENCILS.
WOOF! WOOFF!!
WOOF! WOOFF!!
GRRRRRR...
2

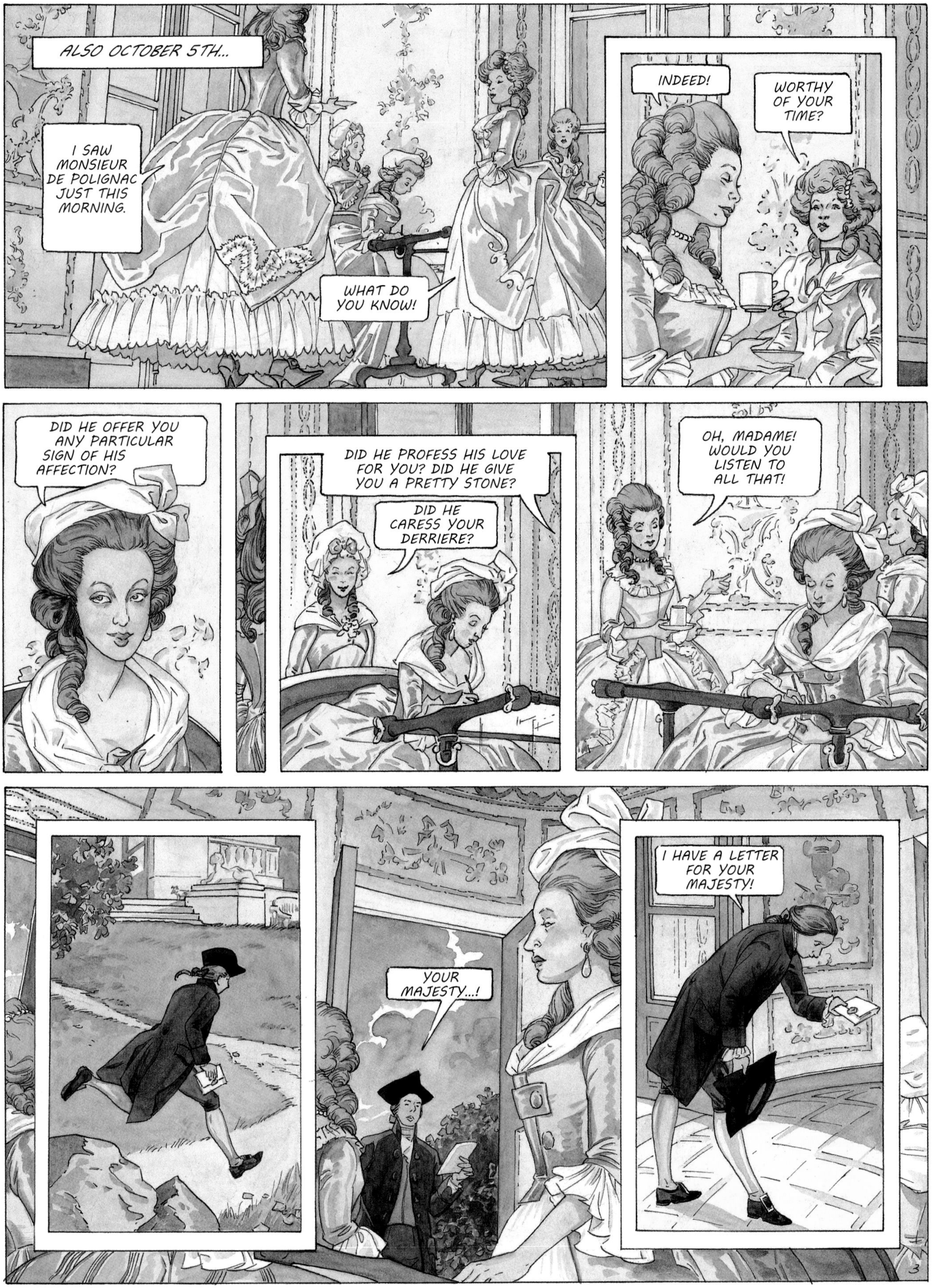
ALSO OCTOBER 5TH...
I SAW MONSIEUR DE POLIGNAC JUST THIS MORNING.
WHAT DO YOU KNOW!
INDEED!
WORTHY OF YOUR TIME?
DID HE OFFER YOU ANY PARTICULAR SIGN OF HIS AFFECTION?
DID HE PROFESS HIS LOVE FOR YOU? DID HE GIVE YOU A PRETTY STONE?
DID HE CARESS YOUR DERRIERE?
OH, MADAME! WOULD YOU LISTEN TO ALL THAT!
YOUR MAJESTY...!
I HAVE A LETTER FOR YOUR MAJESTY!

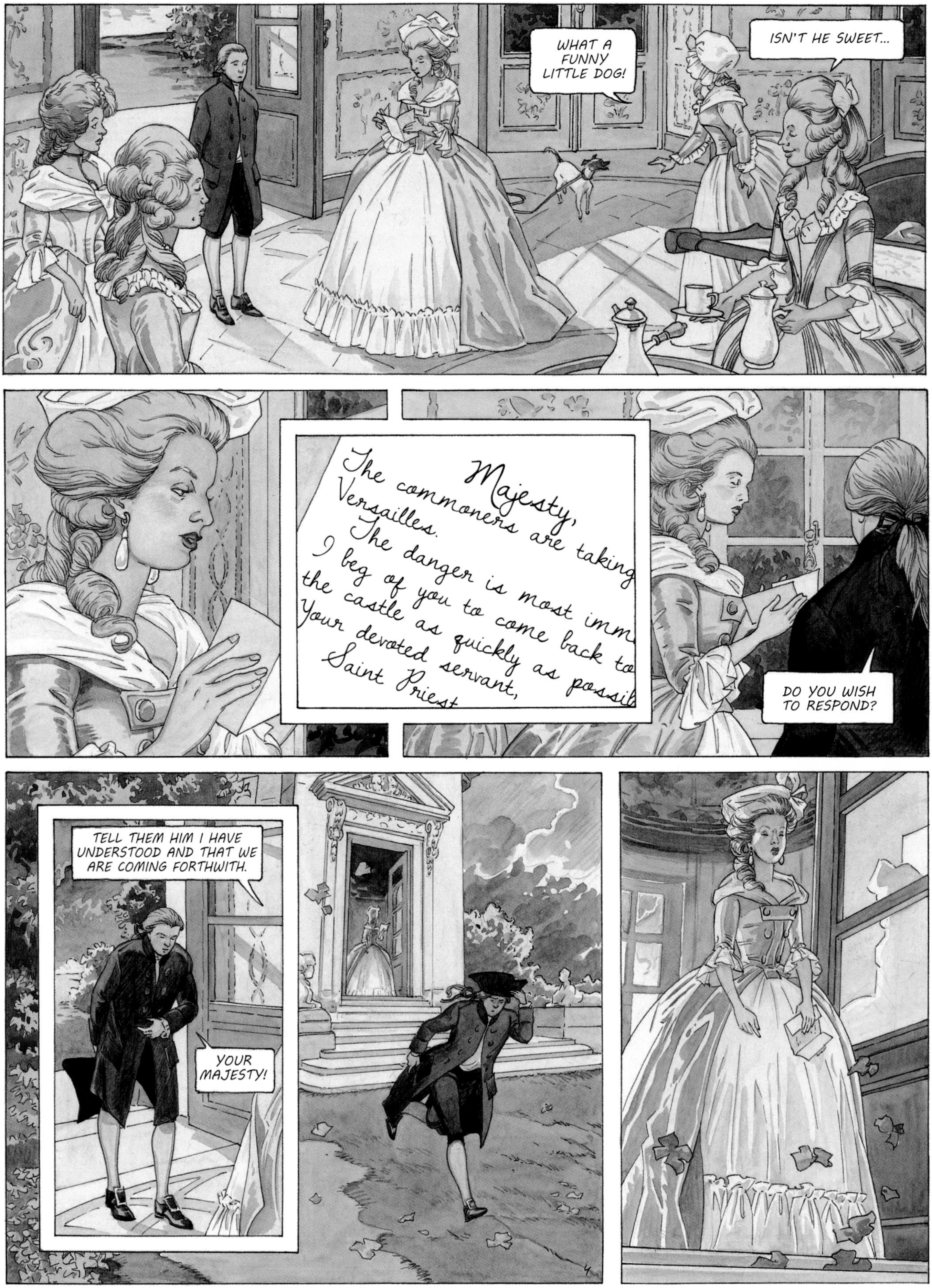
WHAT A FUNNY LITTLE DOG!
ISN'T HE SWEET...
Majesty,
The commoners are taking
Versailles.
The danger is most imm
I beg of you to come back to
the castle as quickly as possib
Your devoted servant,
Saint Priest
DO YOU WISH TO RESPOND?
TELL THEM HIM I HAVE UNDERSTOOD AND THAT WE ARE COMING FORTHWITH.
YOUR MAJESTY!

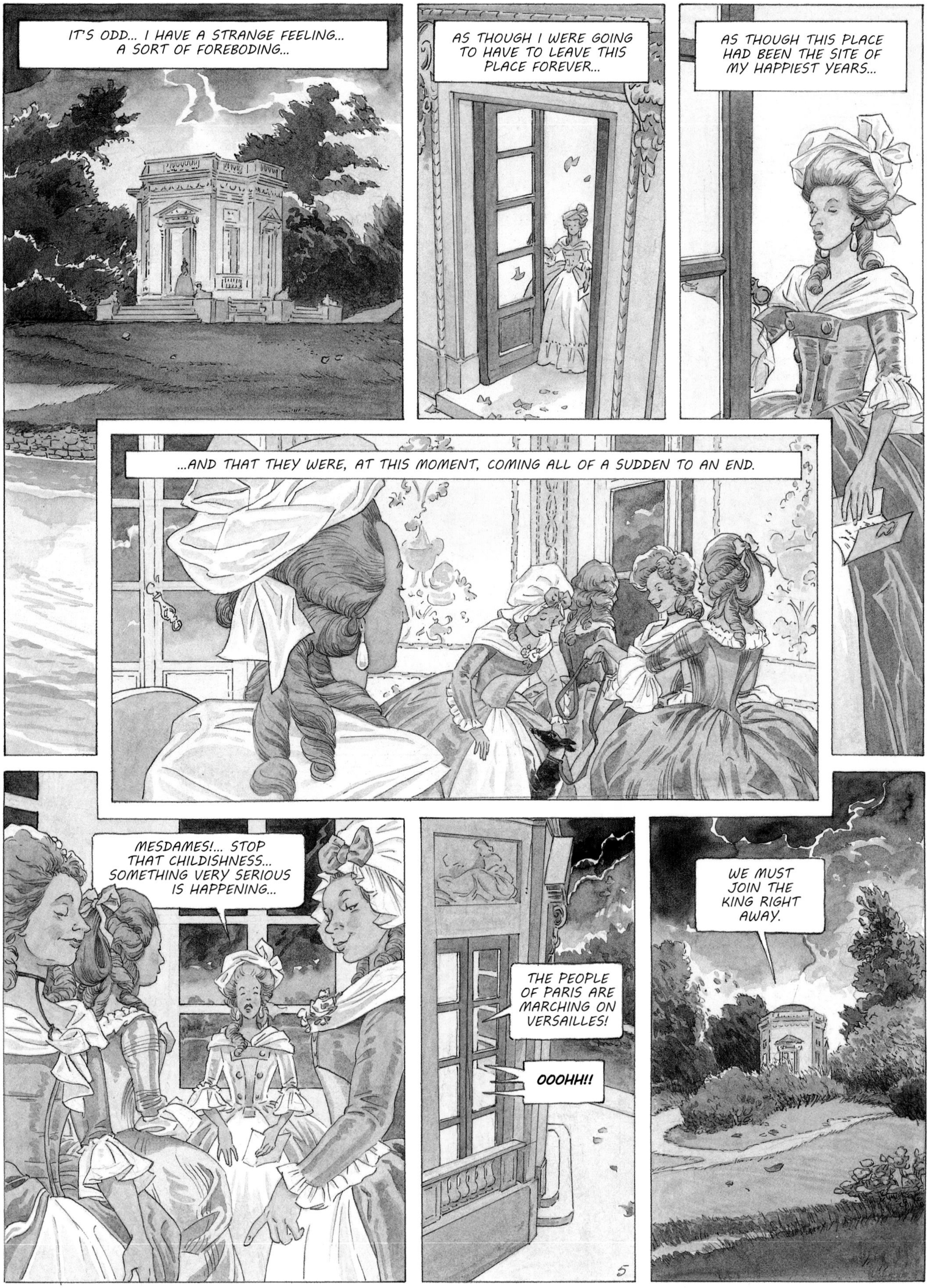
IT'S ODD... I HAVE A STRANGE FEELING... A SORT OF FOREBODING...
AS THOUGH I WERE GOING TO HAVE TO LEAVE THIS PLACE FOREVER...
AS THOUGH THIS PLACE HAD BEEN THE SITE OF MY HAPPIEST YEARS...
...AND THAT THEY WERE, AT THIS MOMENT, COMING ALL OF A SUDDEN TO AN END.
MESDAMES!... STOP THAT CHILDISHNESS... SOMETHING VERY SERIOUS IS HAPPENING...
THE PEOPLE OF PARIS ARE MARCHING ON VERSAILLES!
OOOHH!!
WE MUST JOIN THE KING RIGHT AWAY.

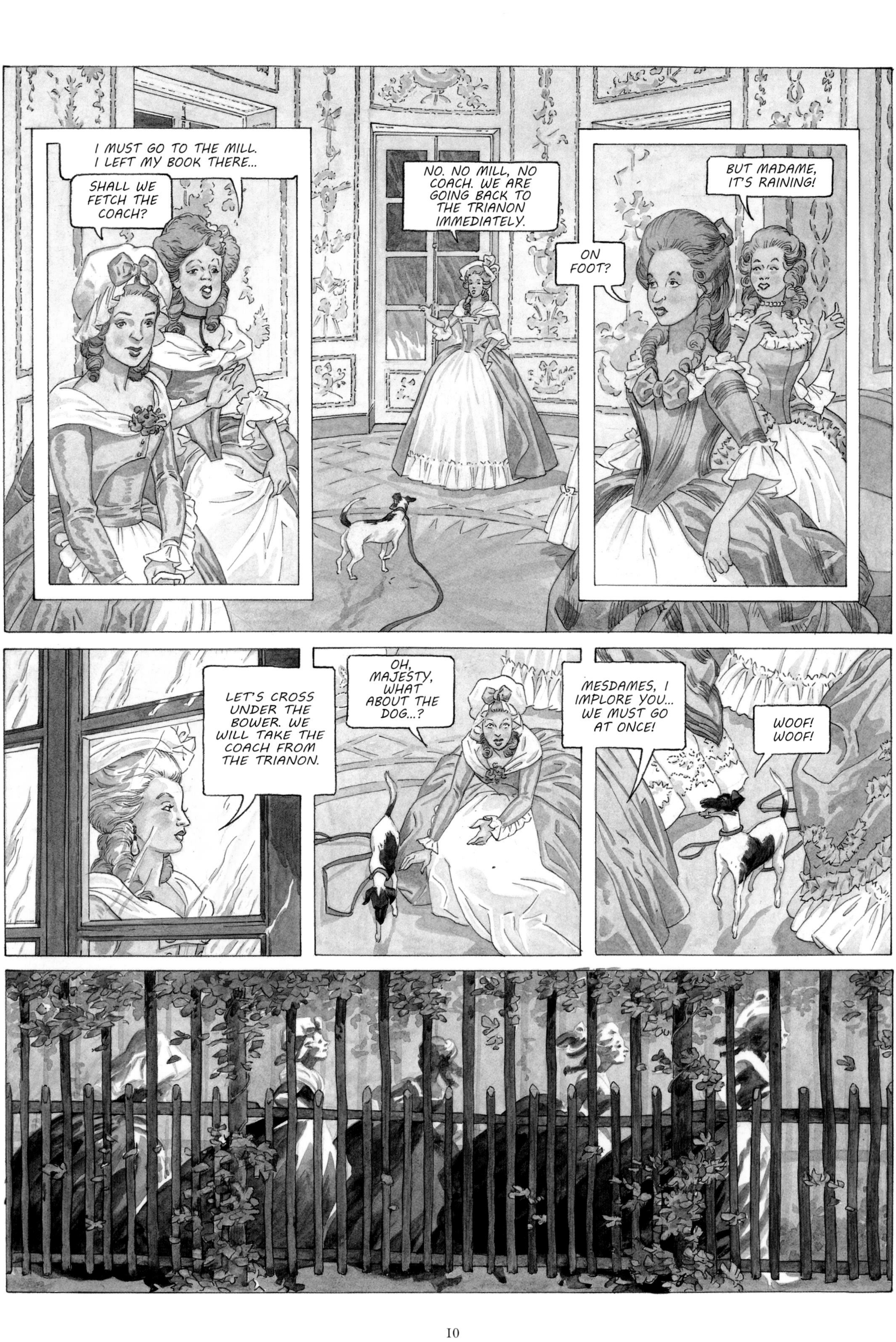
I MUST GO TO THE MILL. I LEFT MY BOOK THERE...
SHALL WE FETCH THE COACH?
NO. NO MILL, NO COACH. WE ARE GOING BACK TO THE TRIANON IMMEDIATELY.
BUT MADAME, IT'S RAINING!
ON FOOT?
LET'S CROSS UNDER THE BOWER. WE WILL TAKE THE COACH FROM THE TRIANON.
OH, MAJESTY, WHAT ABOUT THE DOG...?
MESDAMES, I IMPLORE YOU... WE MUST GO AT ONCE!
WOOF! WOOF!

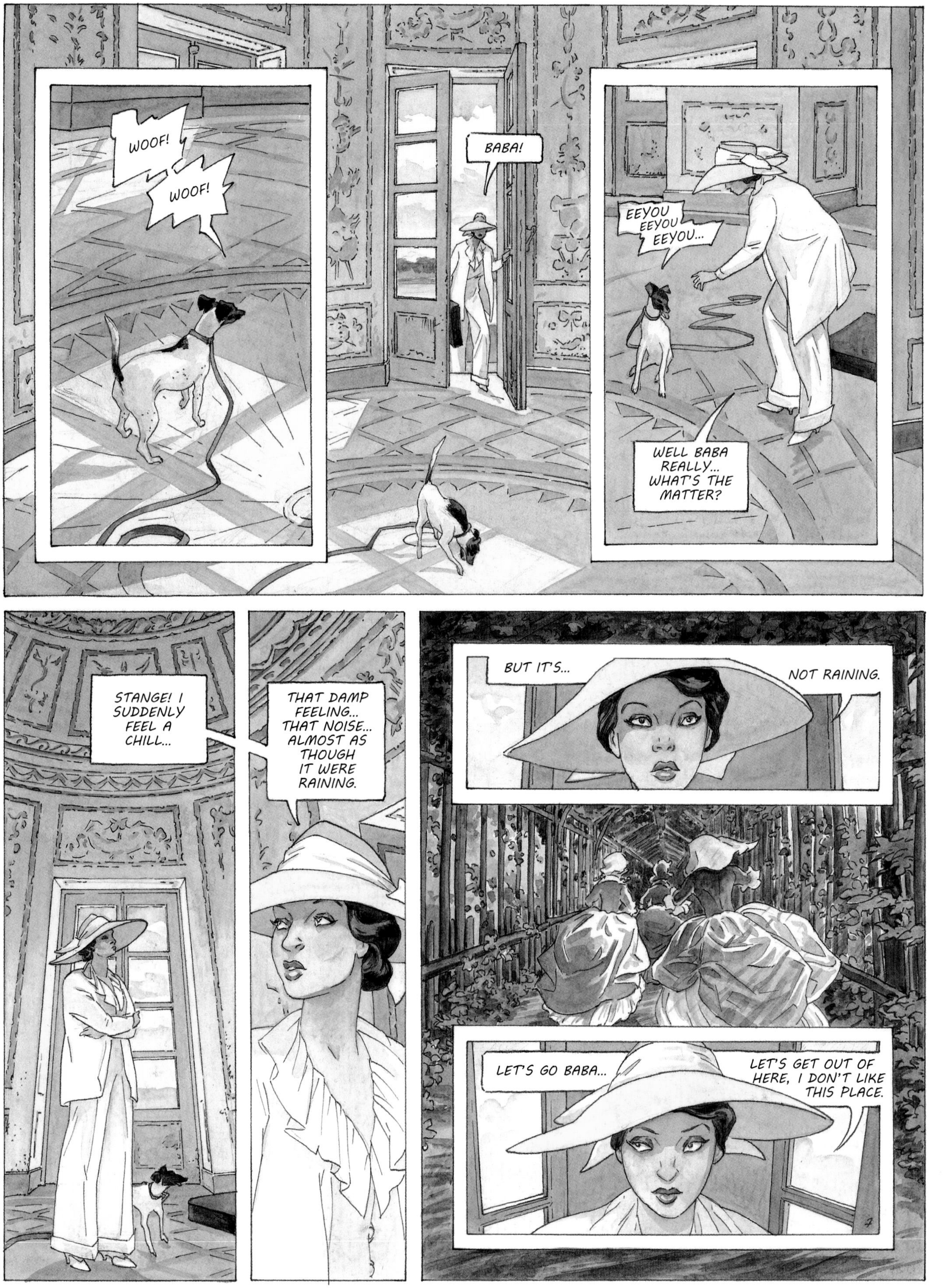
WOOF!
WOOF!
BABA!
EEYOU EEYOU EEYOU...
WELL BABA REALLY... WHAT'S THE MATTER?
STANGE! I SUDDENLY FEEL A CHILL...
THAT DAMP FEELING... THAT NOISE... ALMOST AS THOUGH IT WERE RAINING.
BUT IT'S...
NOT RAINING.
LET'S GO BABA...
LET'S GET OUT OF HERE, I DON'T LIKE THIS PLACE.

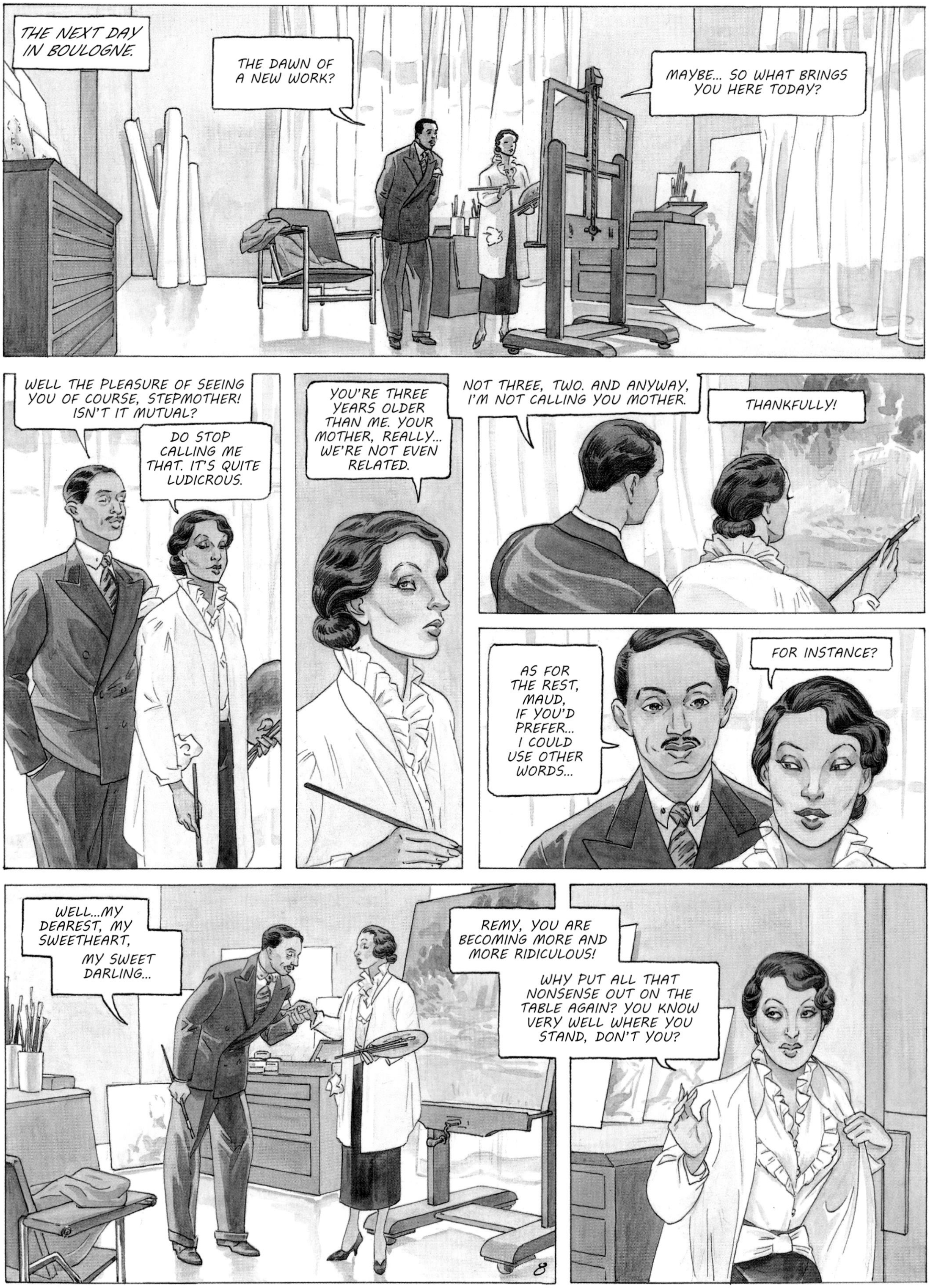
THE NEXT DAY IN BOULOGNE.
THE DAWN OF A NEW WORK?
MAYBE... SO WHAT BRINGS YOU HERE TODAY?
WELL THE PLEASURE OF SEEING YOU OF COURSE, STEPMOTHER! ISN'T IT MUTUAL?
DO STOP CALLING ME THAT. IT'S QUITE LUDICROUS.
YOU'RE THREE YEARS OLDER THAN ME. YOUR MOTHER, REALLY... WE'RE NOT EVEN RELATED.
NOT THREE, TWO. AND ANYWAY, I'M NOT CALLING YOU MOTHER.
THANKFULLY!
AS FOR THE REST, MAUD, IF YOU'D PREFER... I COULD USE OTHER WORDS...
FOR INSTANCE?
WELL...MY DEAREST, MY SWEETHEART, MY SWEET DARLING...
REMY, YOU ARE BECOMING MORE AND MORE RIDICULOUS!
WHY PUT ALL THAT NONSENSE OUT ON THE TABLE AGAIN? YOU KNOW VERY WELL WHERE YOU STAND, DON'T YOU?

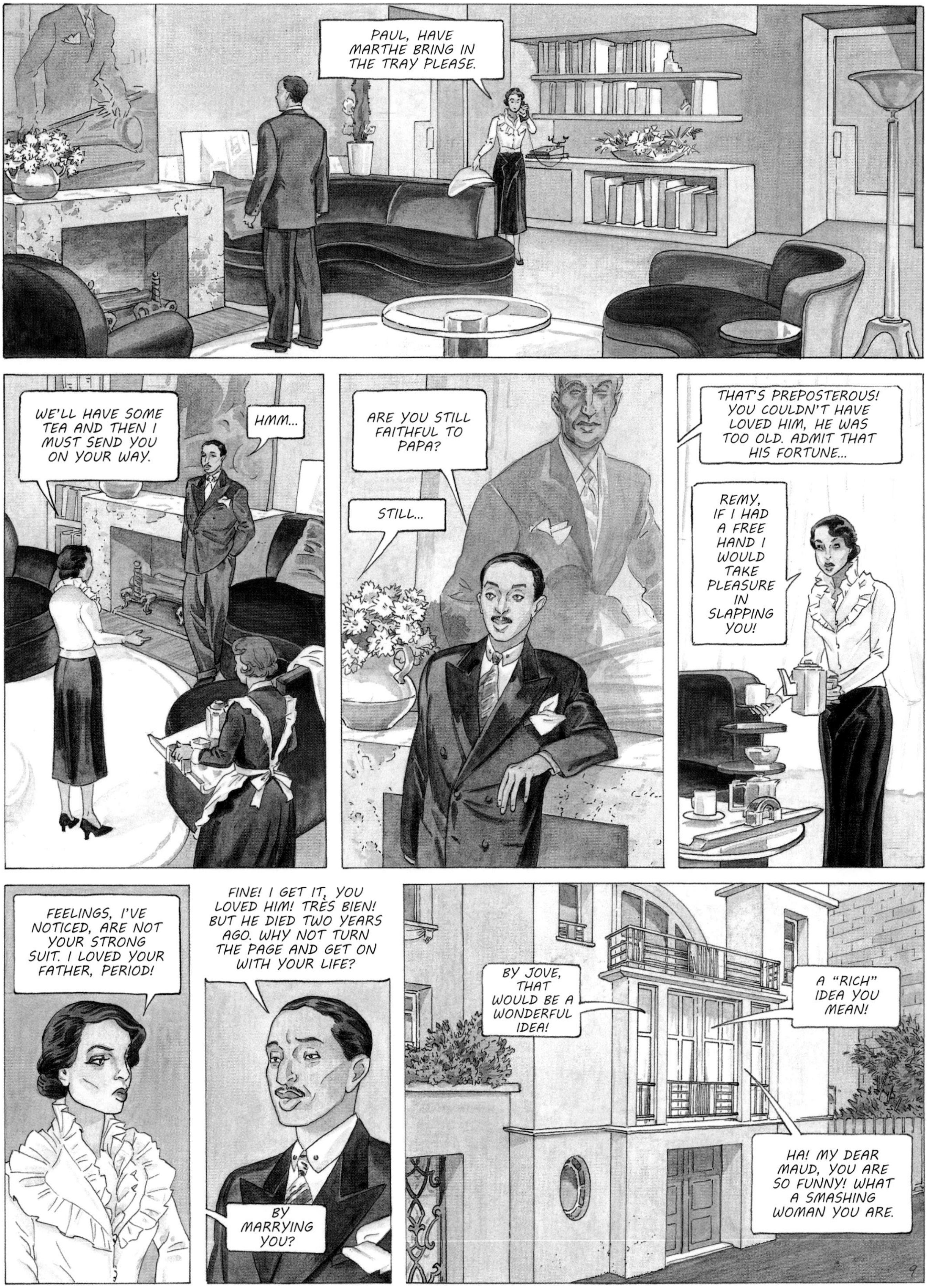

PAUL, HAVE MARTHE BRING IN THE TRAY PLEASE.
WE'LL HAVE SOME TEA AND THEN I MUST SEND YOU ON YOUR WAY.
HMM...
ARE YOU STILL FAITHFUL TO PAPA?
STILL...
THAT'S PREPOSTEROUS! YOU COULDN'T HAVE LOVED HIM, HE WAS TOO OLD. ADMIT THAT HIS FORTUNE...
REMY, IF I HAD A FREE HAND I WOULD TAKE PLEASURE IN SLAPPING YOU!
FEELINGS, I'VE NOTICED, ARE NOT YOUR STRONG SUIT. I LOVED YOUR FATHER, PERIOD!
FINE! I GET IT, YOU LOVED HIM! TRÈS BIEN! BUT HE DIED TWO YEARS AGO. WHY NOT TURN THE PAGE AND GET ON WITH YOUR LIFE?
BY MARRYING YOU?
BY JOVE, THAT WOULD BE A WONDERFUL IDEA!
A "RICH" IDEA YOU MEAN!
HA! MY DEAR MAUD, YOU ARE SO FUNNY! WHAT A SMASHING WOMAN YOU ARE.

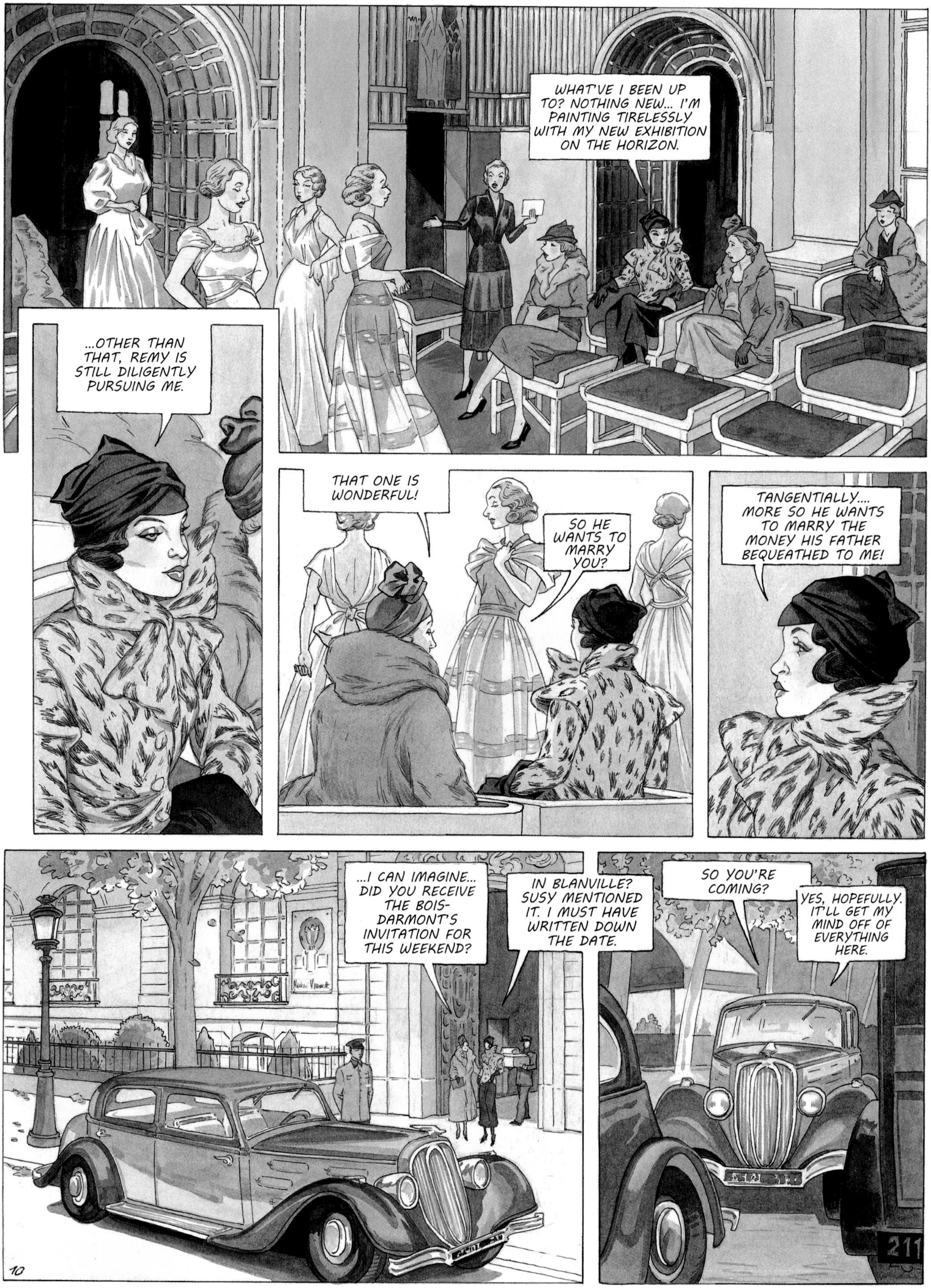
WHAT'VE I BEEN UP TO? NOTHING NEW... I'M PAINTING TIRELESSLY WITH MY NEW EXHIBITION ON THE HORIZON.
...OTHER THAN THAT, REMY IS STILL DILIGENTLY PURSUING ME.
THAT ONE IS WONDERFUL!
SO HE WANTS TO MARRY YOU?
TANGENTIALLY.... MORE SO HE WANTS TO MARRY THE MONEY HIS FATHER BEQUEATHED TO ME!
...I CAN IMAGINE... DID YOU RECEIVE THE BOIS-DARMONT'S INVITATION FOR THIS WEEKEND?
IN BLANVILLE? SUSY MENTIONED IT. I MUST HAVE WRITTEN DOWN THE DATE.
SO YOU'RE COMING?
YES, HOPEFULLY. IT'LL GET MY MIND OFF OF EVERYTHING HERE.
10
211

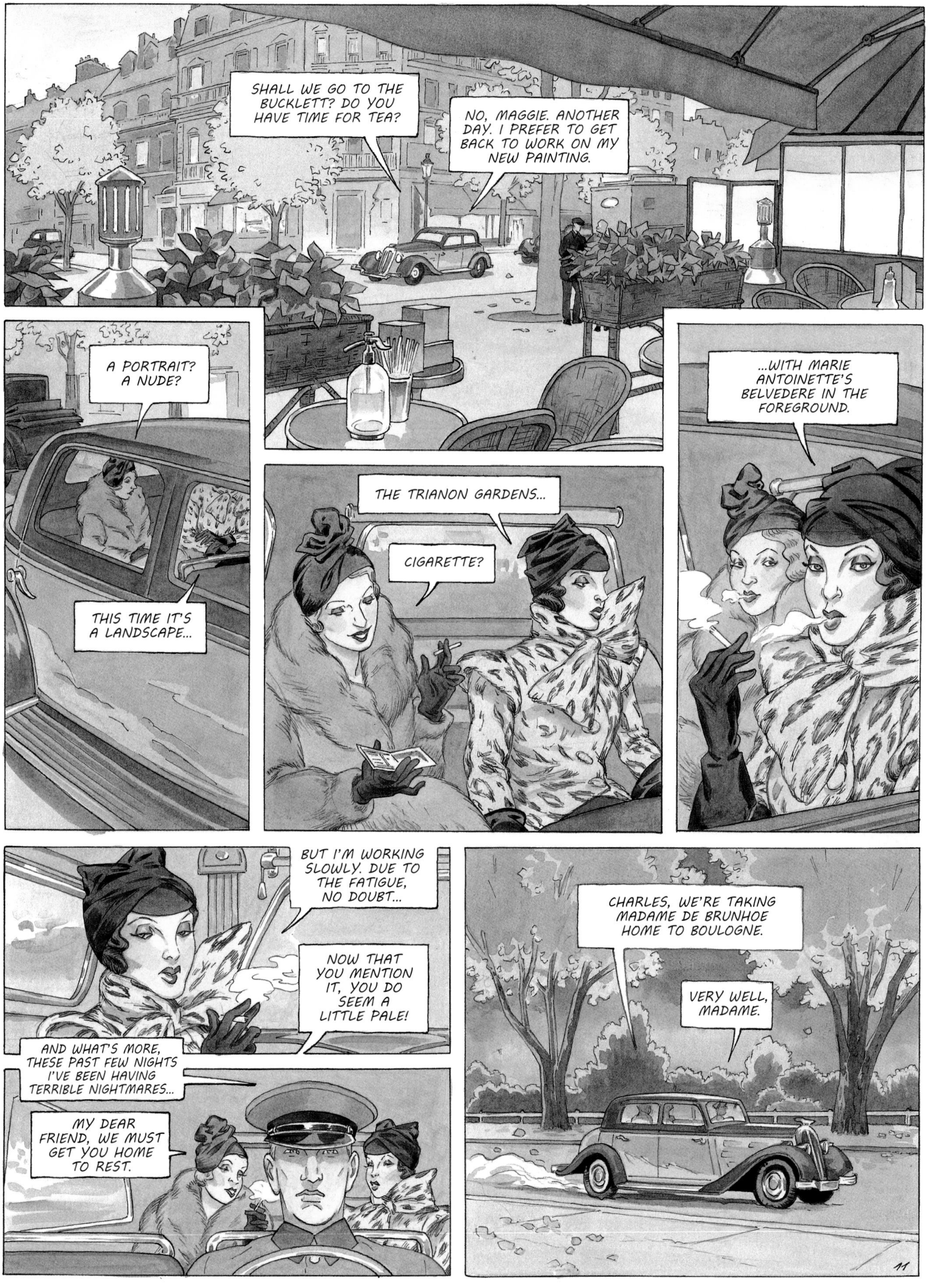
SHALL WE GO TO THE BUCKLETT? DO YOU HAVE TIME FOR TEA?
NO, MAGGIE. ANOTHER DAY. I PREFER TO GET BACK TO WORK ON MY NEW PAINTING.
A PORTRAIT? A NUDE?
THIS TIME IT'S A LANDSCAPE...
THE TRIANON GARDENS...
CIGARETTE?
...WITH MARIE ANTOINETTE'S BELVEDERE IN THE FOREGROUND.
BUT I'M WORKING SLOWLY. DUE TO THE FATIGUE, NO DOUBT...
NOW THAT YOU MENTION IT, YOU DO SEEM A LITTLE PALE!
AND WHAT'S MORE, THESE PAST FEW NIGHTS I'VE BEEN HAVING TERRIBLE NIGHTMARES...
MY DEAR FRIEND, WE MUST GET YOU HOME TO REST.
CHARLES, WE'RE TAKING MADAME DE BRUNHOE HOME TO BOULOGNE.
VERY WELL, MADAME.
11

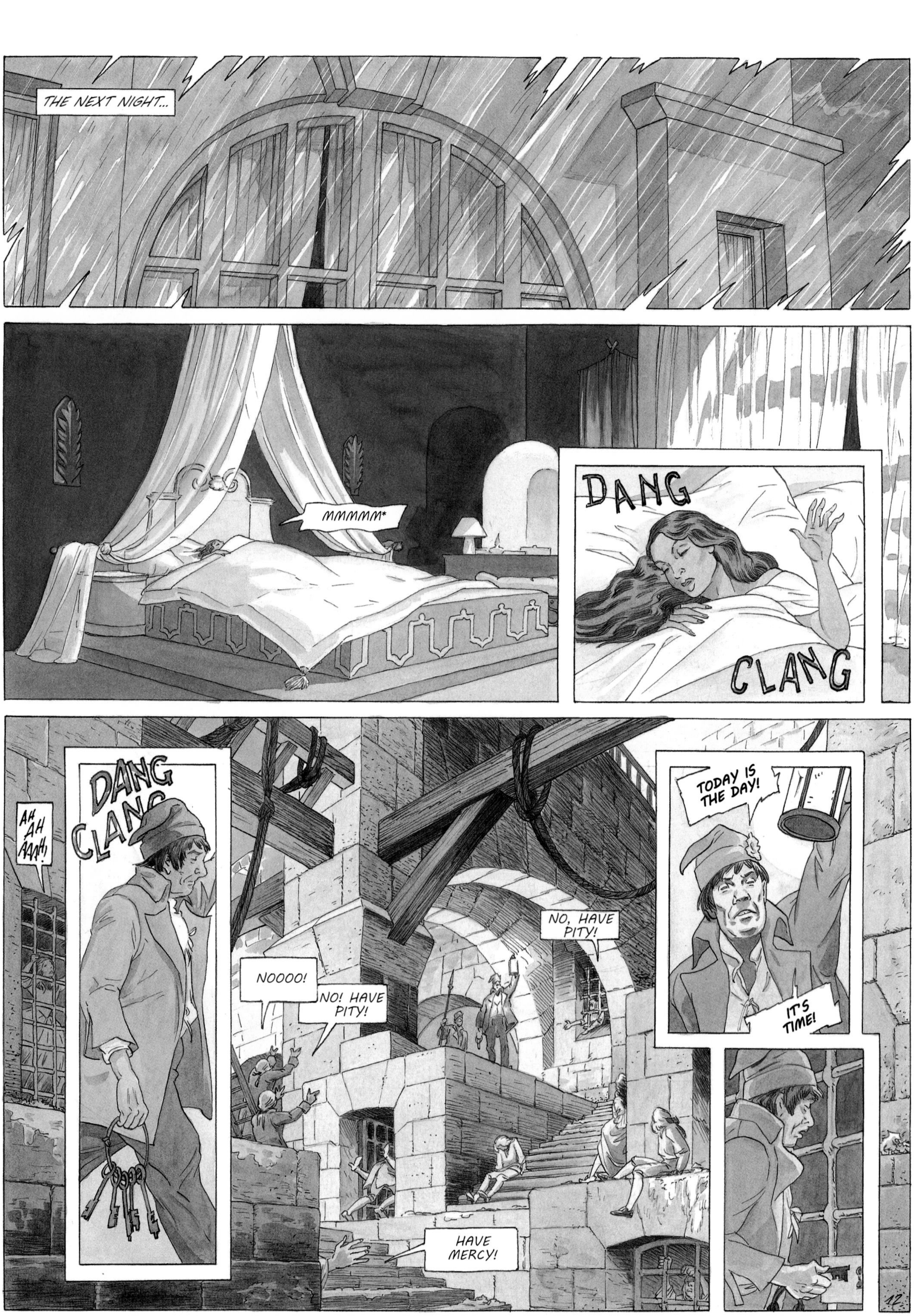

THE NEXT NIGHT...
MMMMM*
DANG
CLANG
DANG
CLANG
AH AH AAAH!
NOOOO!
NO! HAVE PITY!
NO, HAVE PITY!
HAVE MERCY!
TODAY IS THE DAY!
IT'S TIME!
12

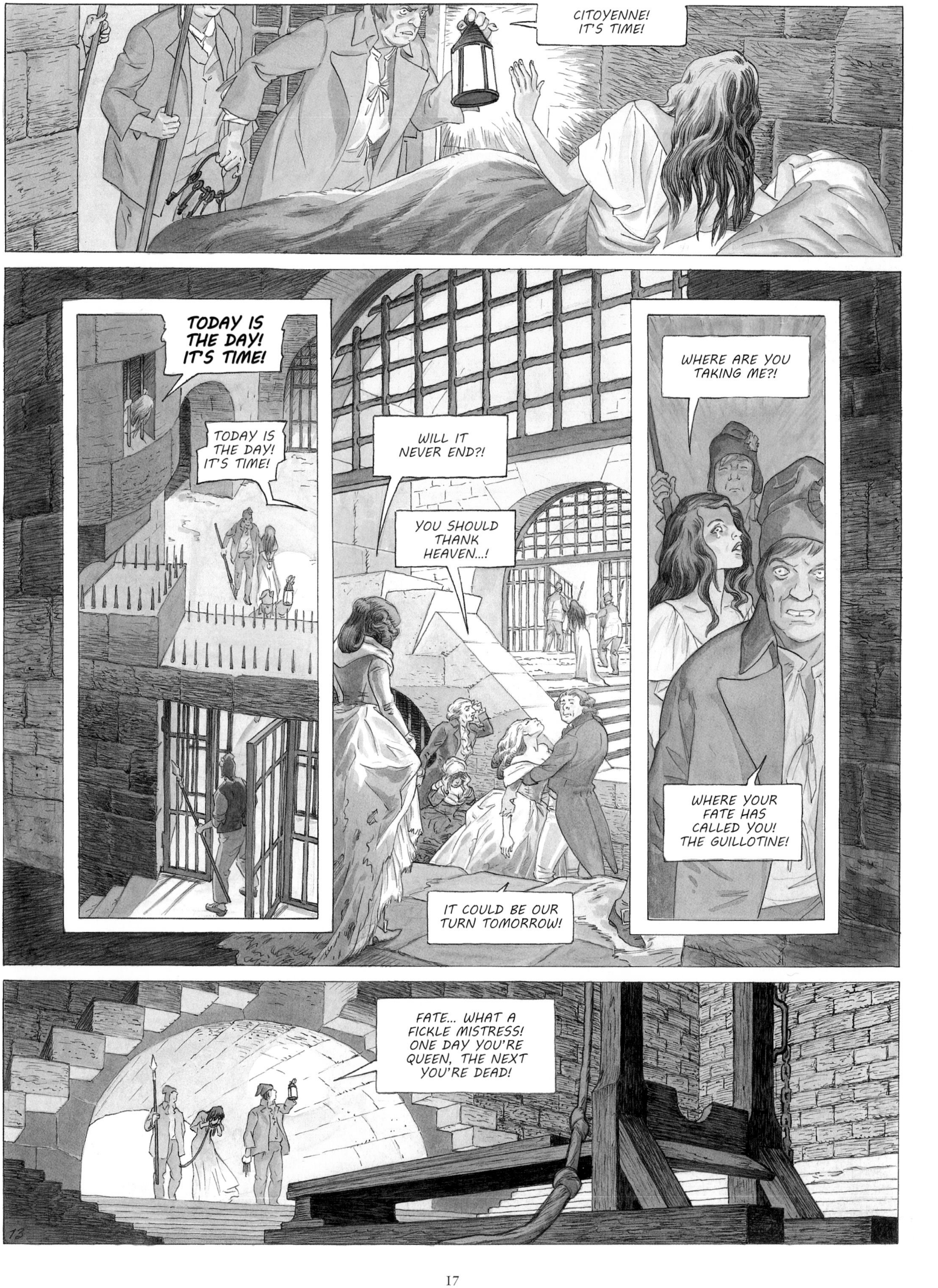
CITOYENNE! IT'S TIME!
TODAY IS THE DAY! IT'S TIME!
TODAY IS THE DAY! IT'S TIME!
WILL IT NEVER END?!
YOU SHOULD THANK HEAVEN...!
IT COULD BE OUR TURN TOMORROW!
WHERE ARE YOU TAKING ME?!
WHERE YOUR FATE HAS CALLED YOU! THE GUILLOTINE!
FATE... WHAT A FICKLE MISTRESS! ONE DAY YOU'RE QUEEN, THE NEXT YOU'RE DEAD!

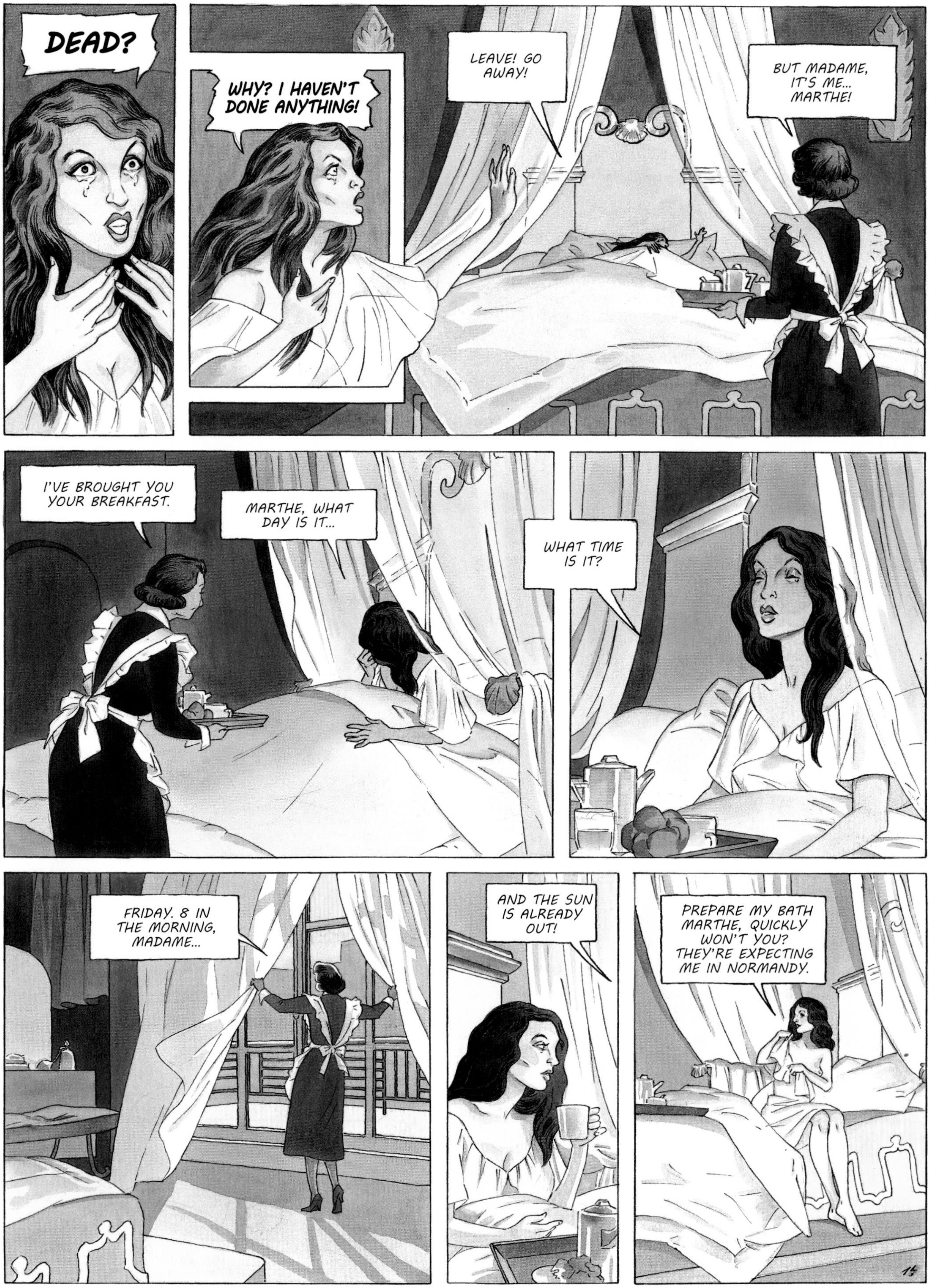
DEAD?
WHY? I HAVEN'T DONE ANYTHING!
LEAVE! GO AWAY!
BUT MADAME, IT'S ME... MARTHE!
I'VE BROUGHT YOU YOUR BREAKFAST.
MARTHE, WHAT DAY IS IT...
WHAT TIME IS IT?
FRIDAY. 8 IN THE MORNING, MADAME...
AND THE SUN IS ALREADY OUT!
PREPARE MY BATH MARTHE, QUICKLY WON'T YOU? THEY'RE EXPECTING ME IN NORMANDY.
14

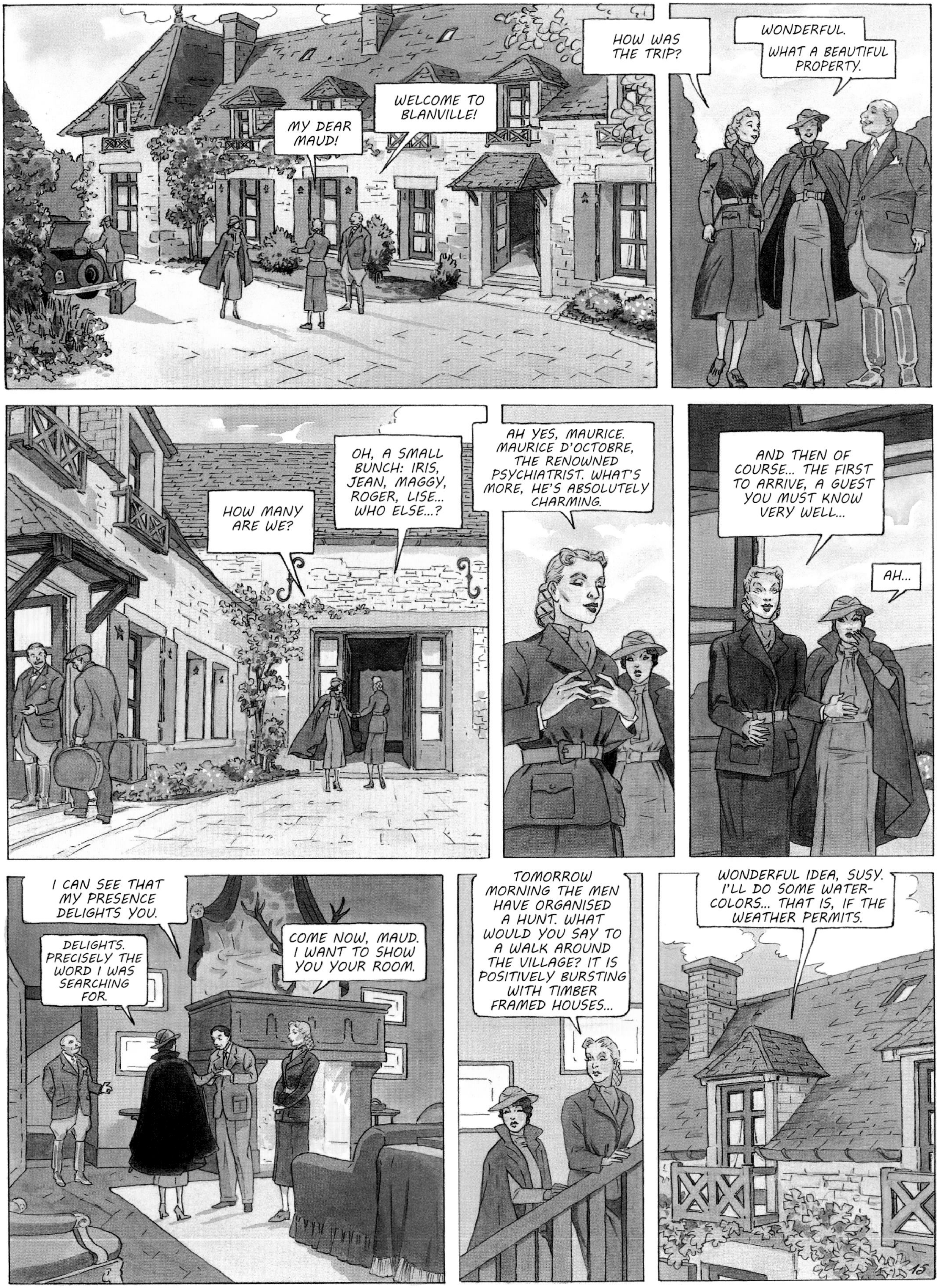
MY DEAR MAUD!
WELCOME TO BLANVILLE!
HOW WAS THE TRIP?
WONDERFUL.
WHAT A BEAUTIFUL PROPERTY.
HOW MANY ARE WE?
OH, A SMALL BUNCH: IRIS, JEAN, MAGGY, ROGER, LISE... WHO ELSE...?
AH YES, MAURICE. MAURICE D'OCTOBRE, THE RENOWNED PSYCHIATRIST. WHAT'S MORE, HE'S ABSOLUTELY CHARMING.
AND THEN OF COURSE... THE FIRST TO ARRIVE, A GUEST YOU MUST KNOW VERY WELL...
AH...
I CAN SEE THAT MY PRESENCE DELIGHTS YOU.
DELIGHTS. PRECISELY THE WORD I WAS SEARCHING FOR.
COME NOW, MAUD. I WANT TO SHOW YOU YOUR ROOM.
TOMORROW MORNING THE MEN HAVE ORGANISED A HUNT. WHAT WOULD YOU SAY TO A WALK AROUND THE VILLAGE? IT IS POSITIVELY BURSTING WITH TIMBER FRAMED HOUSES...
WONDERFUL IDEA, SUSY. I'LL DO SOME WATER-COLORS... THAT IS, IF THE WEATHER PERMITS.
15

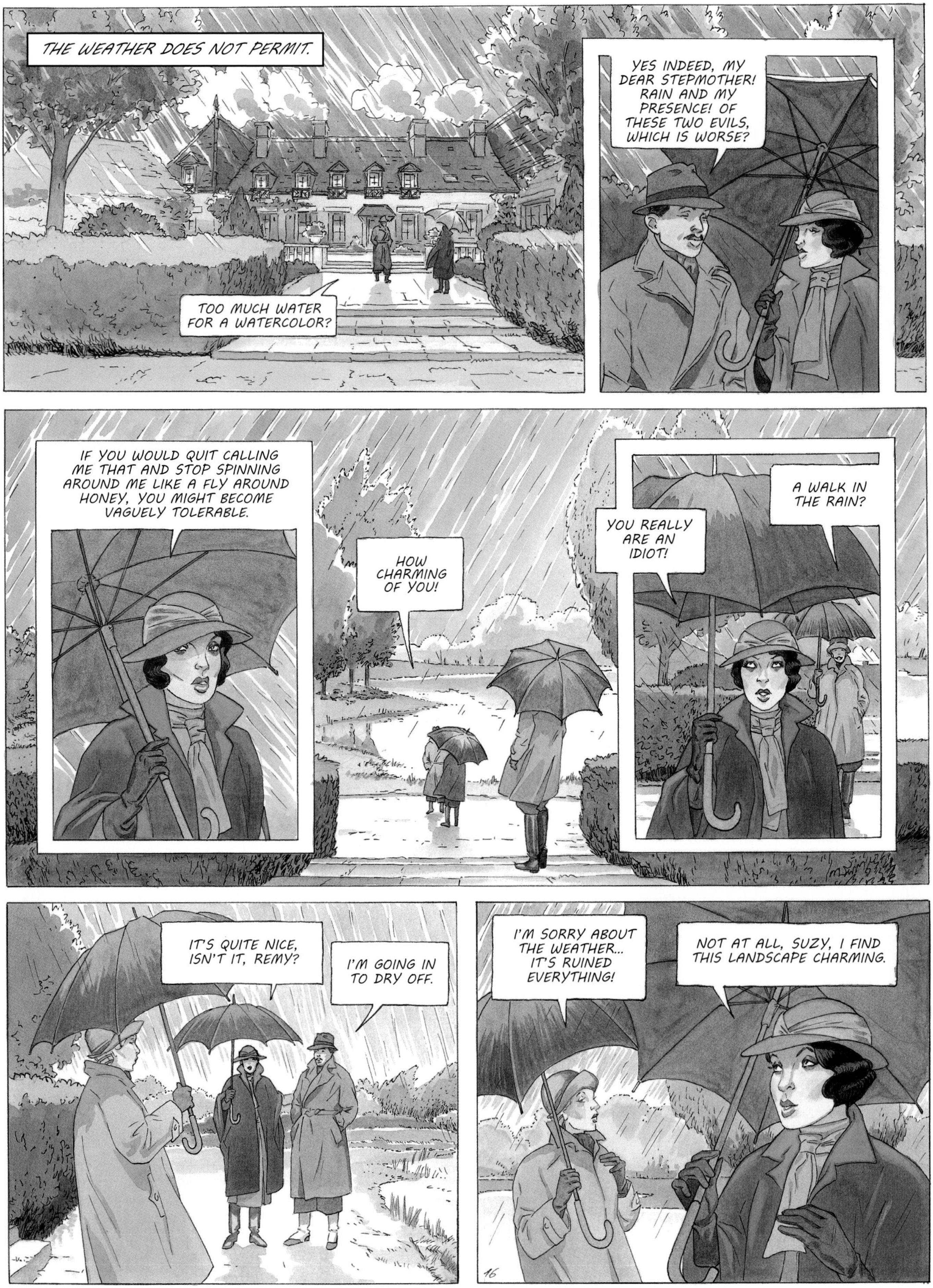
THE WEATHER DOES NOT PERMIT.
TOO MUCH WATER FOR A WATERCOLOR?
YES INDEED, MY DEAR STEPMOTHER! RAIN AND MY PRESENCE! OF THESE TWO EVILS, WHICH IS WORSE?
IF YOU WOULD QUIT CALLING ME THAT AND STOP SPINNING AROUND ME LIKE A FLY AROUND HONEY, YOU MIGHT BECOME VAGUELY TOLERABLE.
HOW CHARMING OF YOU!
A WALK IN THE RAIN?
YOU REALLY ARE AN IDIOT!
IT'S QUITE NICE, ISN'T IT, REMY?
I'M GOING IN TO DRY OFF.
I'M SORRY ABOUT THE WEATHER... IT'S RUINED EVERYTHING!
NOT AT ALL, SUZY, I FIND THIS LANDSCAPE CHARMING.

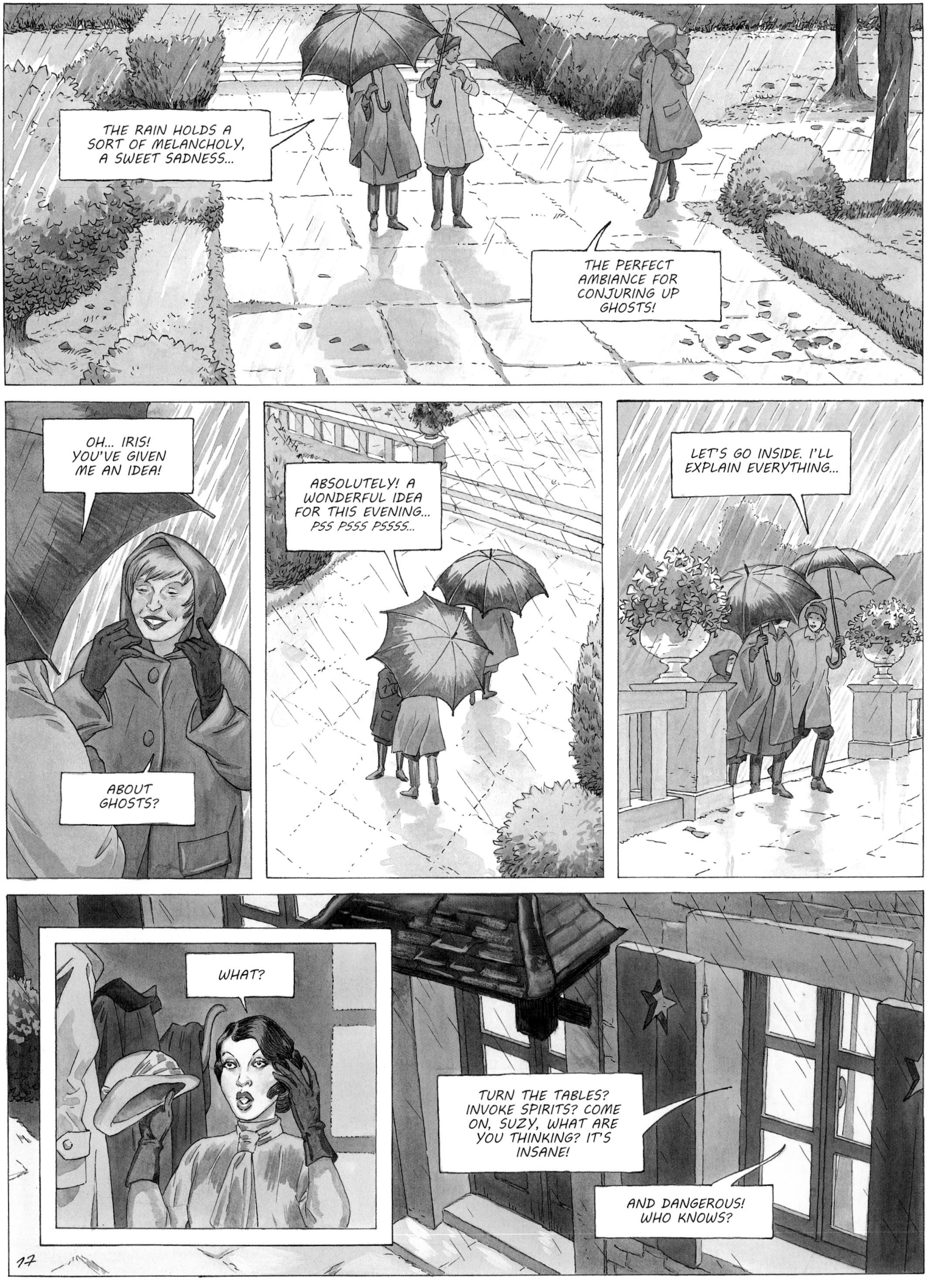
THE RAIN HOLDS A SORT OF MELANCHOLY, A SWEET SADNESS...
THE PERFECT AMBIANCE FOR CONJURING UP GHOSTS!
OH... IRIS! YOU'VE GIVEN ME AN IDEA!
ABOUT GHOSTS?
ABSOLUTELY! A WONDERFUL IDEA FOR THIS EVENING... PSS PSSS PSSSS...
LET'S GO INSIDE. I'LL EXPLAIN EVERYTHING...
WHAT?
TURN THE TABLES? INVOKE SPIRITS? COME ON, SUZY, WHAT ARE YOU THINKING? IT'S INSANE!
AND DANGEROUS! WHO KNOWS?
17

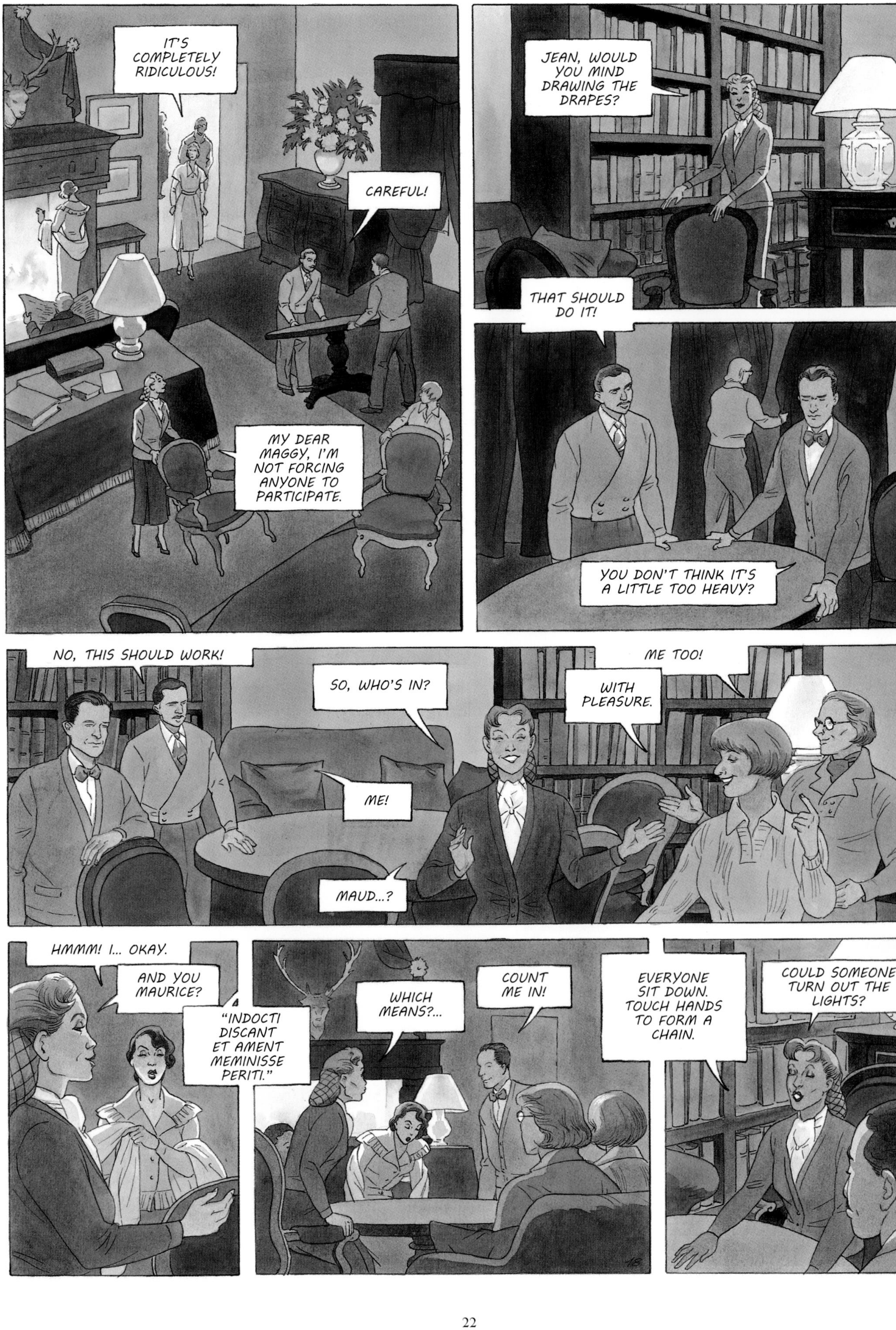
IT'S COMPLETELY RIDICULOUS!
CAREFUL!
MY DEAR MAGGY, I'M NOT FORCING ANYONE TO PARTICIPATE.
JEAN, WOULD YOU MIND DRAWING THE DRAPES?
THAT SHOULD DO IT!
YOU DON'T THINK IT'S A LITTLE TOO HEAVY?
NO, THIS SHOULD WORK!
SO, WHO'S IN?
ME!
MAUD...?
WITH PLEASURE.
ME TOO!
HMMM! I... OKAY.
AND YOU MAURICE?
"INDOCTI DISCANT ET AMENT MEMINISSE PERITI."
WHICH MEANS?...
COUNT ME IN!
EVERYONE SIT DOWN. TOUCH HANDS TO FORM A CHAIN.
COULD SOMEONE TURN OUT THE LIGHTS?

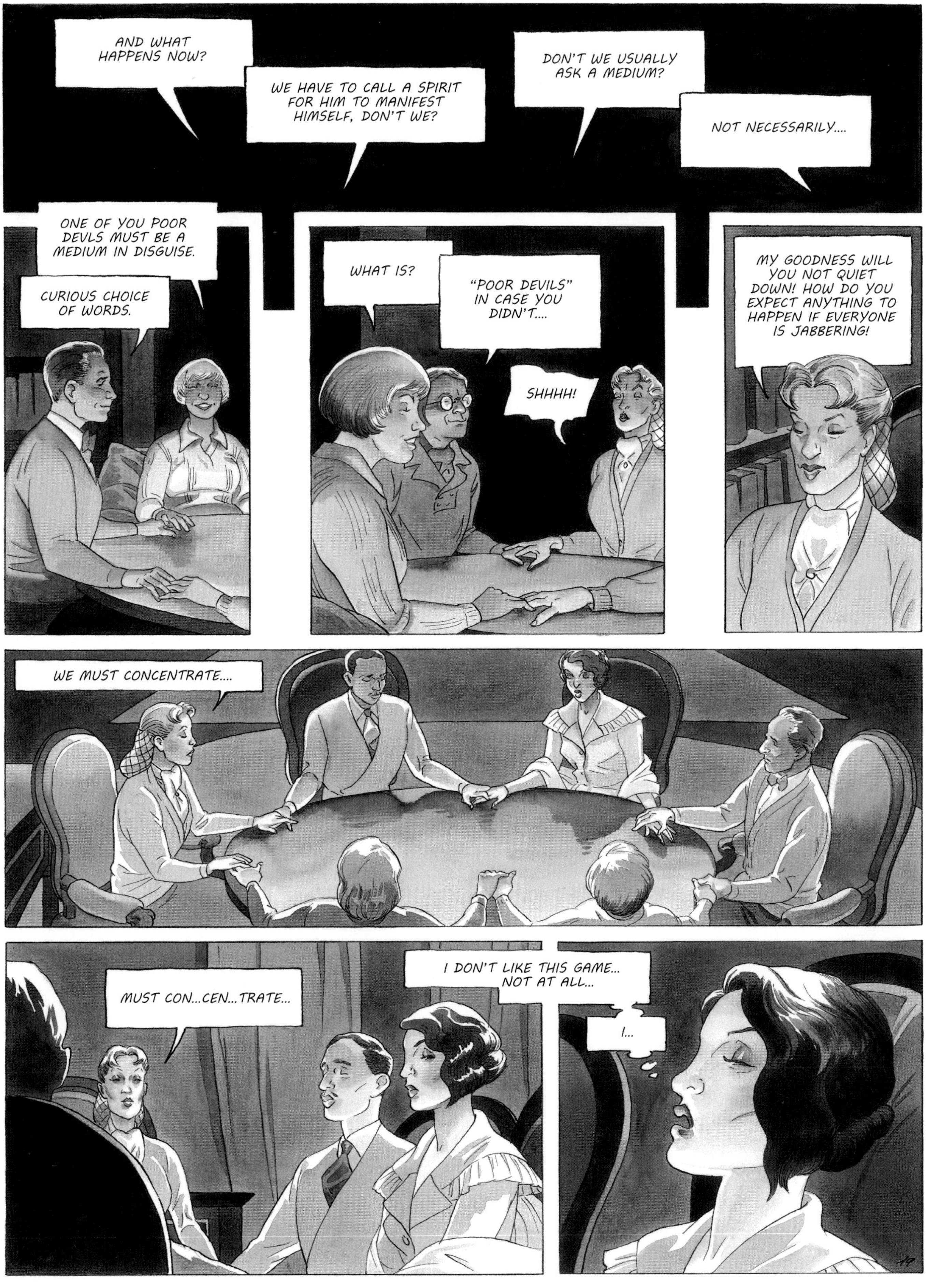
AND WHAT HAPPENS NOW?
WE HAVE TO CALL A SPIRIT FOR HIM TO MANIFEST HIMSELF, DON'T WE?
DON'T WE USUALLY ASK A MEDIUM?
NOT NECESSARILY....
ONE OF YOU POOR DEVLS MUST BE A MEDIUM IN DISGUISE.
CURIOUS CHOICE OF WORDS.
WHAT IS?
"POOR DEVILS" IN CASE YOU DIDN'T....
SHHHH!
MY GOODNESS WILL YOU NOT QUIET DOWN! HOW DO YOU EXPECT ANYTHING TO HAPPEN IF EVERYONE IS JABBERING!
WE MUST CONCENTRATE....
MUST CON...CEN...TRATE...
I DON'T LIKE THIS GAME... NOT AT ALL...
I...

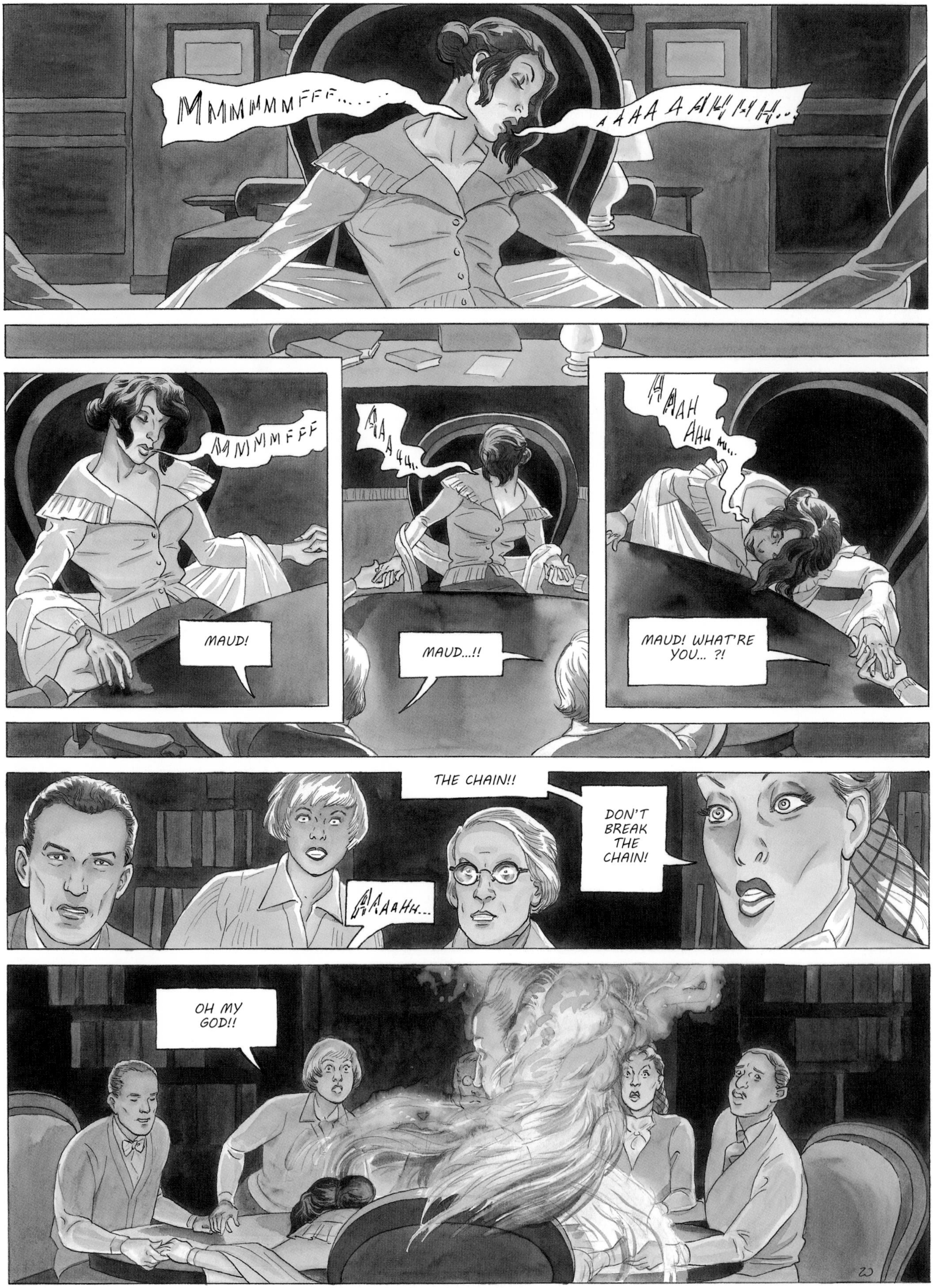
MMMMMMFFF......
AAAAAAHHHH...
MMMMFFF
AAAAHH...
AAAH AHH AH...
MAUD!
MAUD...!!
MAUD! WHAT'RE YOU... ?!
THE CHAIN!!
AAAAHH...
DON'T BREAK THE CHAIN!
OH MY GOD!!

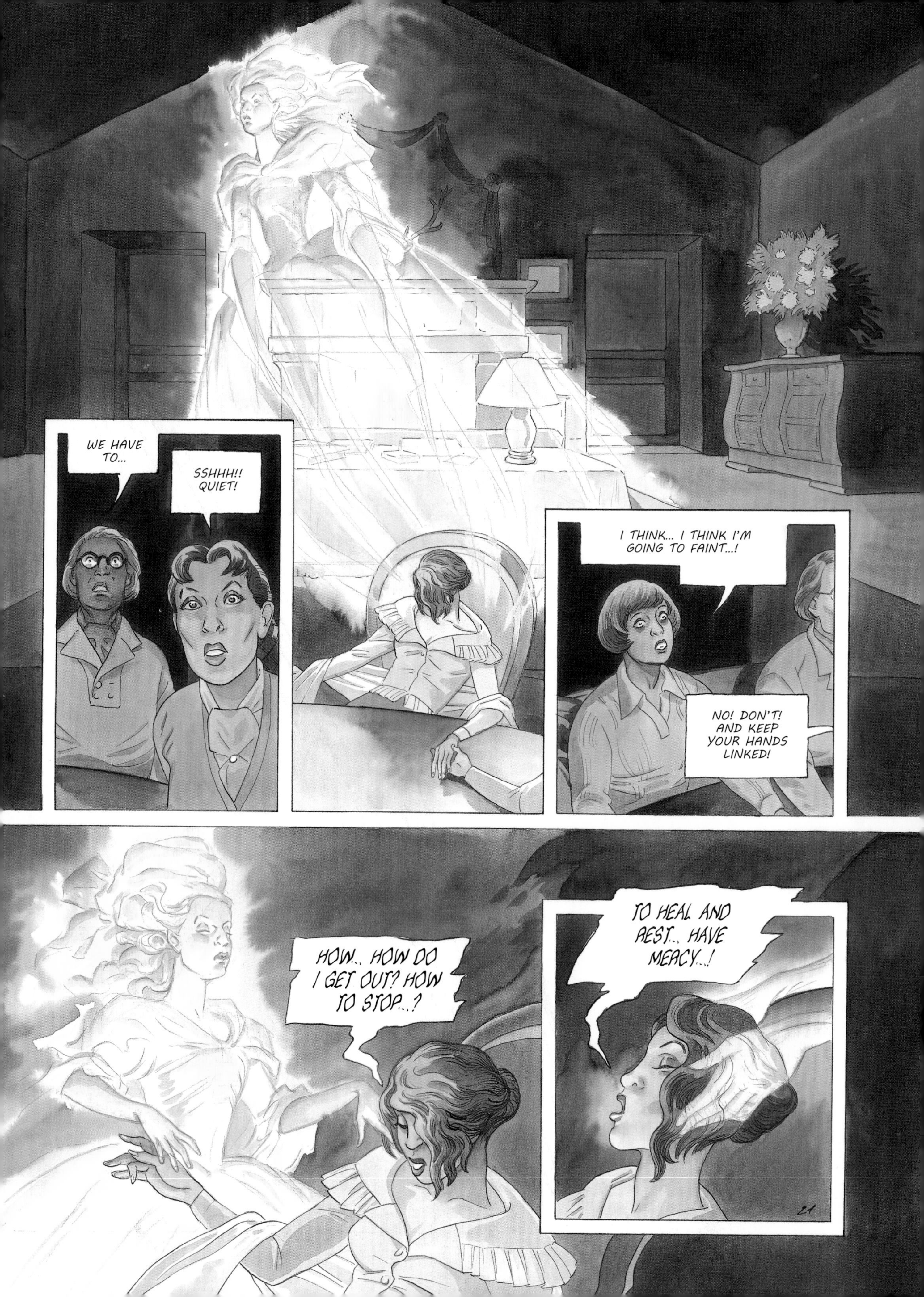

WE HAVE TO...
SSHHH!! QUIET!
I THINK... I THINK I'M GOING TO FAINT...!
NO! DON'T! AND KEEP YOUR HANDS LINKED!
HOW.. HOW DO I GET OUT? HOW TO STOP...?
TO HEAL AND REST... HAVE MERCY...!

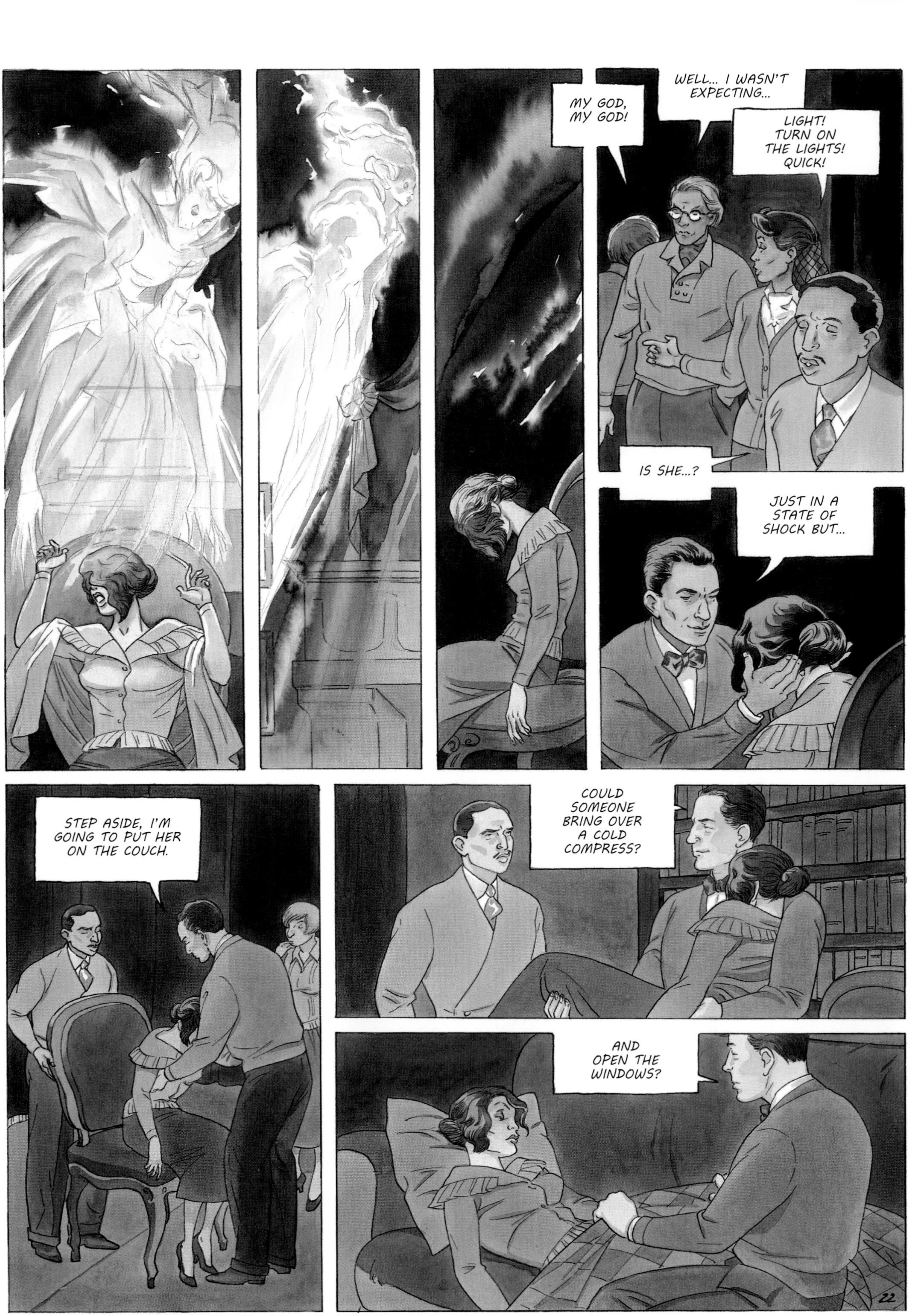
MY GOD, MY GOD!
WELL... I WASN'T EXPECTING...
LIGHT! TURN ON THE LIGHTS! QUICK!
IS SHE...?
JUST IN A STATE OF SHOCK BUT...
STEP ASIDE, I'M GOING TO PUT HER ON THE COUCH.
COULD SOMEONE BRING OVER A COLD COMPRESS?
AND OPEN THE WINDOWS?
22

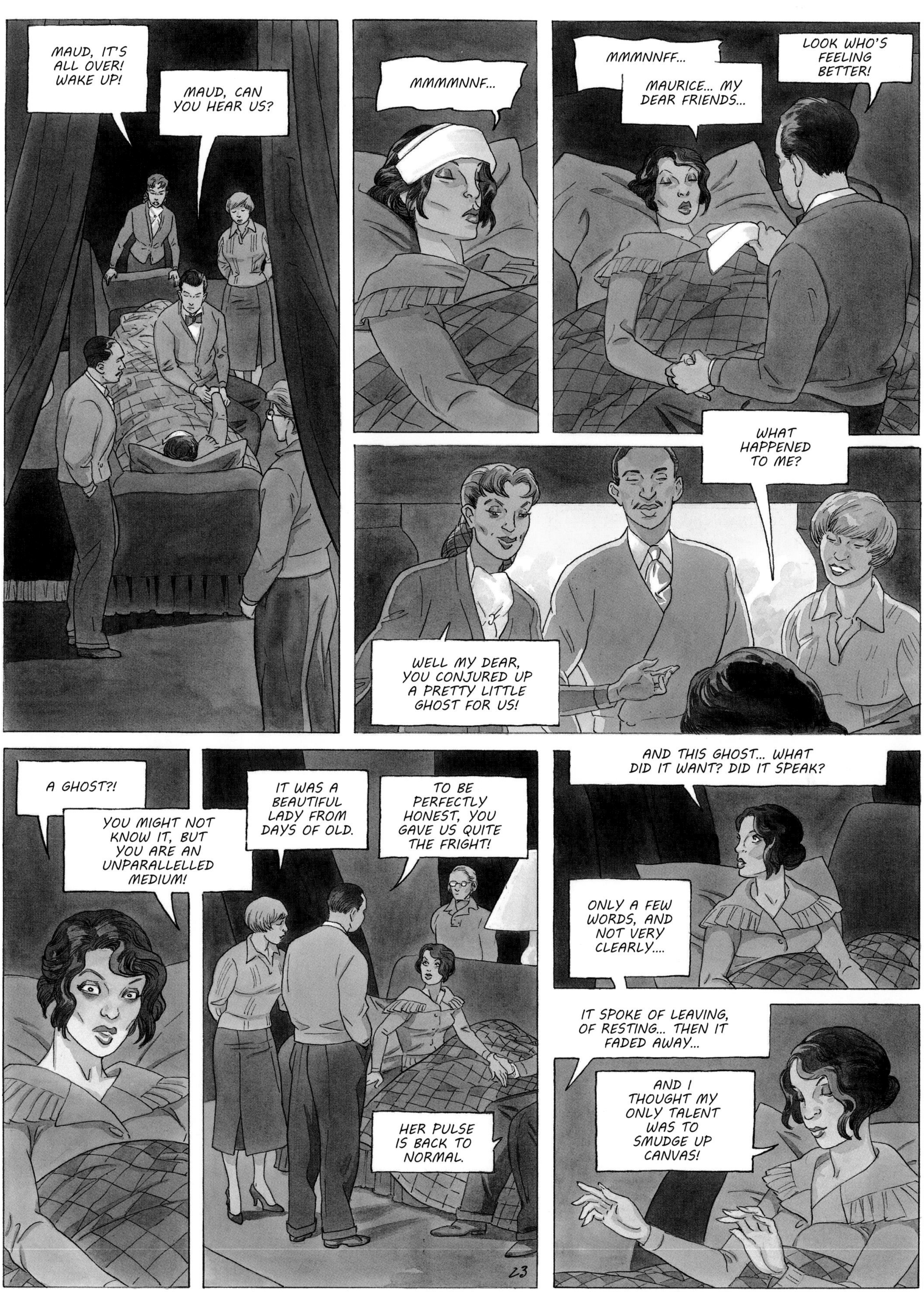
MAUD, IT'S ALL OVER! WAKE UP!
MAUD, CAN YOU HEAR US?
MMMMNNF...
MMMNNFF...
MAURICE... MY DEAR FRIENDS...
LOOK WHO'S FEELING BETTER!
WHAT HAPPENED TO ME?
WELL MY DEAR, YOU CONJURED UP A PRETTY LITTLE GHOST FOR US!
A GHOST?!
YOU MIGHT NOT KNOW IT, BUT YOU ARE AN UNPARALLELLED MEDIUM!
IT WAS A BEAUTIFUL LADY FROM DAYS OF OLD.
TO BE PERFECTLY HONEST, YOU GAVE US QUITE THE FRIGHT!
HER PULSE IS BACK TO NORMAL.
23
AND THIS GHOST... WHAT DID IT WANT? DID IT SPEAK?
ONLY A FEW WORDS, AND NOT VERY CLEARLY....
IT SPOKE OF LEAVING, OF RESTING... THEN IT FADED AWAY...
AND I THOUGHT MY ONLY TALENT WAS TO SMUDGE UP CANVAS!

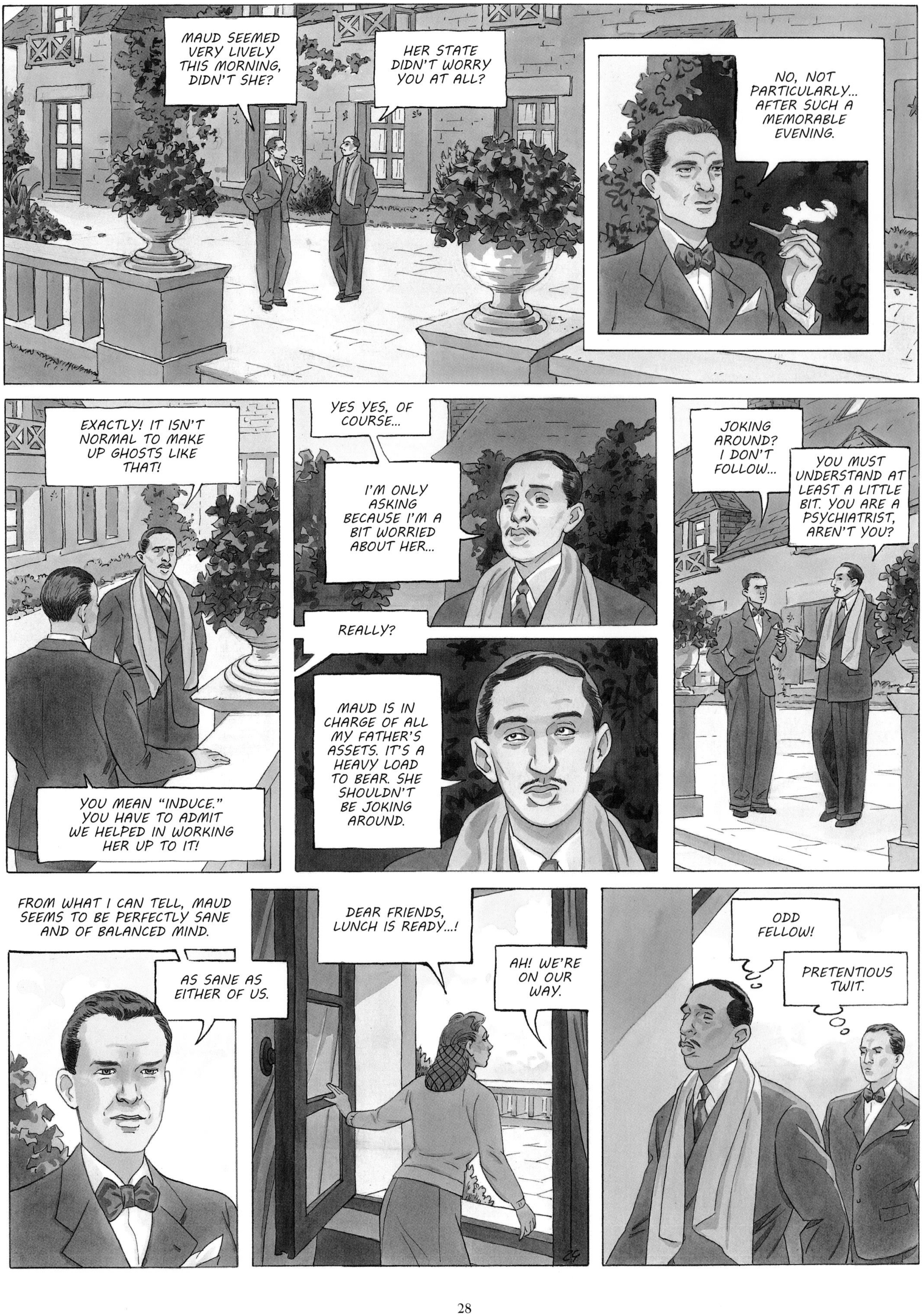
MAUD SEEMED VERY LIVELY THIS MORNING, DIDN'T SHE?
HER STATE DIDN'T WORRY YOU AT ALL?
NO, NOT PARTICULARLY... AFTER SUCH A MEMORABLE EVENING.
EXACTLY! IT ISN'T NORMAL TO MAKE UP GHOSTS LIKE THAT!
YOU MEAN "INDUCE." YOU HAVE TO ADMIT WE HELPED IN WORKING HER UP TO IT!
YES YES, OF COURSE...
I'M ONLY ASKING BECAUSE I'M A BIT WORRIED ABOUT HER...
REALLY?
MAUD IS IN CHARGE OF ALL MY FATHER'S ASSETS. IT'S A HEAVY LOAD TO BEAR. SHE SHOULDN'T BE JOKING AROUND.
JOKING AROUND? I DON'T FOLLOW...
YOU MUST UNDERSTAND AT LEAST A LITTLE BIT. YOU ARE A PSYCHIATRIST, AREN'T YOU?
FROM WHAT I CAN TELL, MAUD SEEMS TO BE PERFECTLY SANE AND OF BALANCED MIND.
AS SANE AS EITHER OF US.
DEAR FRIENDS, LUNCH IS READY...!
AH! WE'RE ON OUR WAY.
ODD FELLOW!
PRETENTIOUS TWIT.

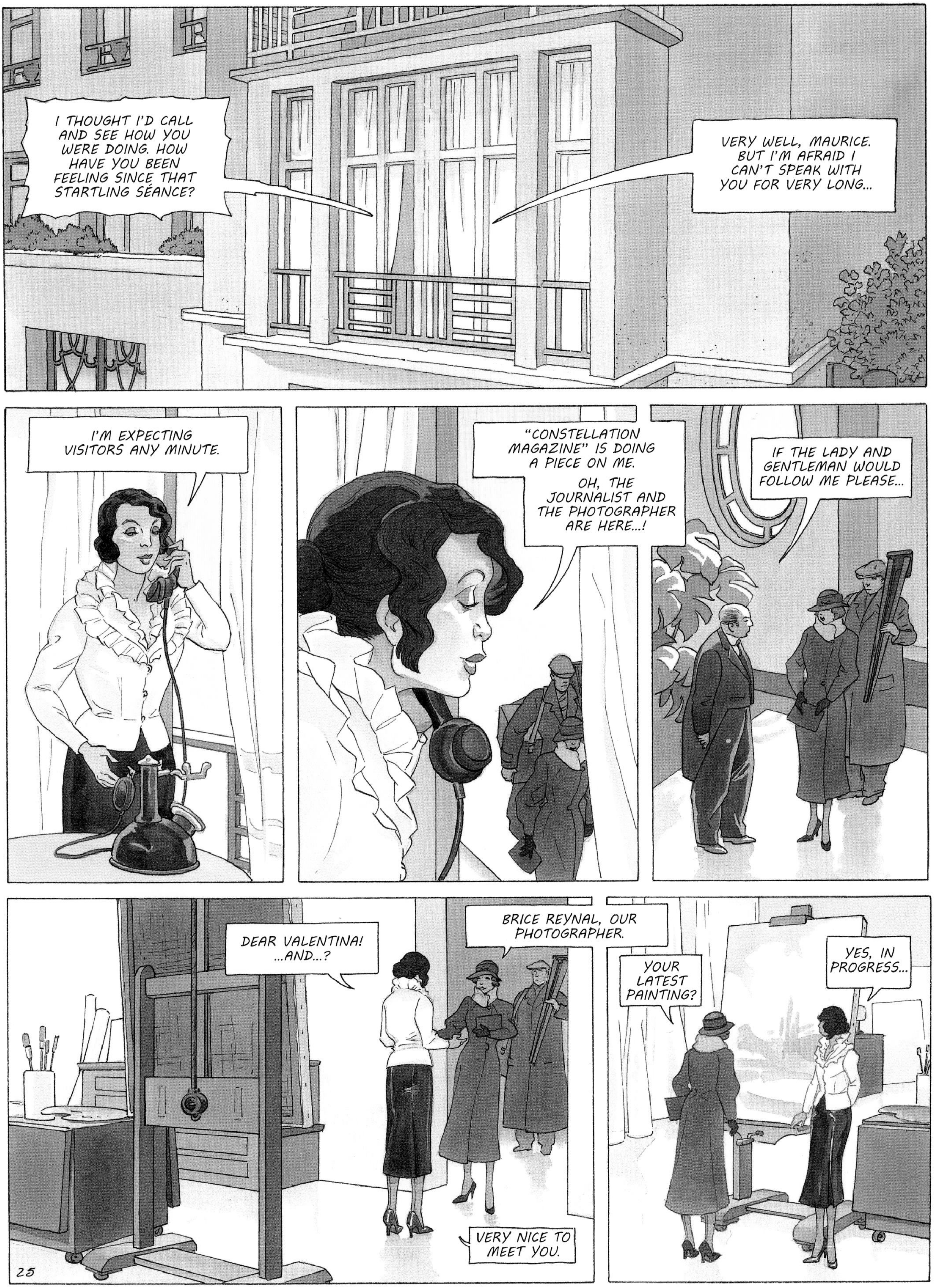
I THOUGHT I'D CALL AND SEE HOW YOU WERE DOING. HOW HAVE YOU BEEN FEELING SINCE THAT STARTLING SÉANCE?
VERY WELL, MAURICE. BUT I'M AFRAID I CAN'T SPEAK WITH YOU FOR VERY LONG...
I'M EXPECTING VISITORS ANY MINUTE.
"CONSTELLATION MAGAZINE" IS DOING A PIECE ON ME.
OH, THE JOURNALIST AND THE PHOTOGRAPHER ARE HERE...!
IF THE LADY AND GENTLEMAN WOULD FOLLOW ME PLEASE...
DEAR VALENTINA! ...AND...?
BRICE REYNAL, OUR PHOTOGRAPHER.
VERY NICE TO MEET YOU.
YOUR LATEST PAINTING?
YES, IN PROGRESS...
25

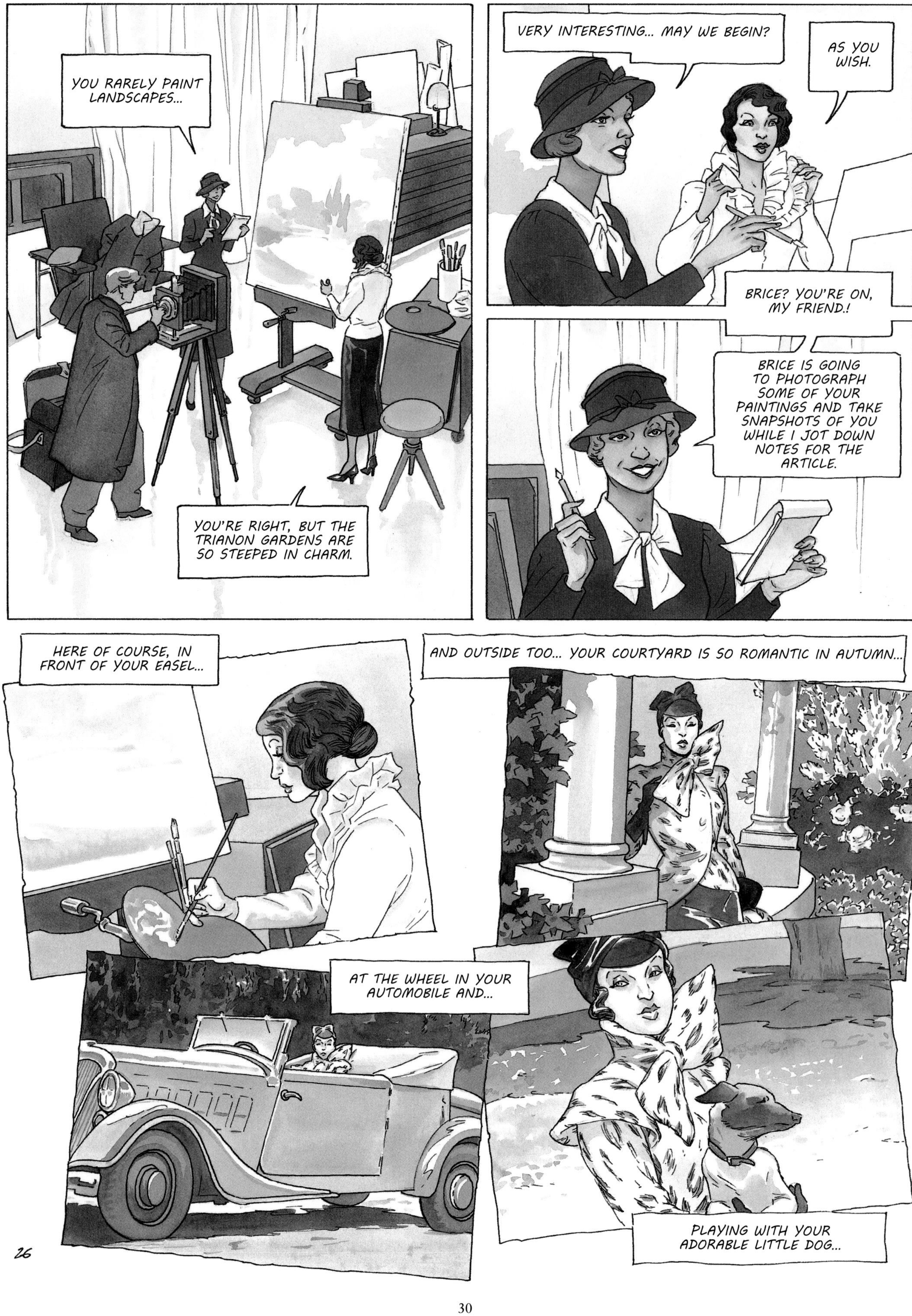

YOU RARELY PAINT LANDSCAPES...
YOU'RE RIGHT, BUT THE TRIANON GARDENS ARE SO STEEPED IN CHARM.
VERY INTERESTING... MAY WE BEGIN?
AS YOU WISH.
BRICE? YOU'RE ON, MY FRIEND.!
BRICE IS GOING TO PHOTOGRAPH SOME OF YOUR PAINTINGS AND TAKE SNAPSHOTS OF YOU WHILE I JOT DOWN NOTES FOR THE ARTICLE.
HERE OF COURSE, IN FRONT OF YOUR EASEL...
AND OUTSIDE TOO... YOUR COURTYARD IS SO ROMANTIC IN AUTUMN...
AT THE WHEEL IN YOUR AUTOMOBILE AND...
PLAYING WITH YOUR ADORABLE LITTLE DOG...
26

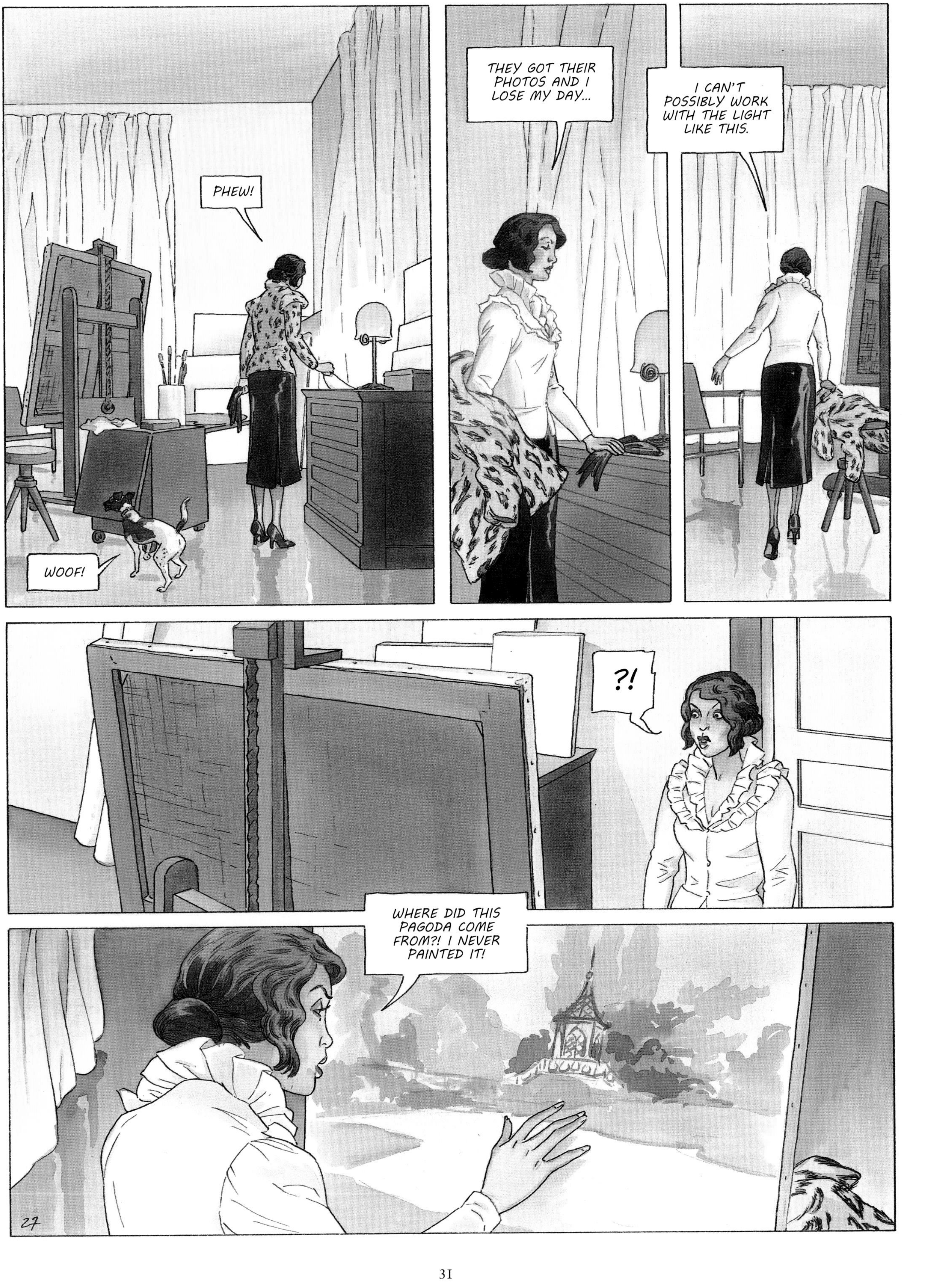
PHEW!
WOOF!
THEY GOT THEIR PHOTOS AND I LOSE MY DAY...
I CAN'T POSSIBLY WORK WITH THE LIGHT LIKE THIS.
?!
WHERE DID THIS PAGODA COME FROM?! I NEVER PAINTED IT!
27

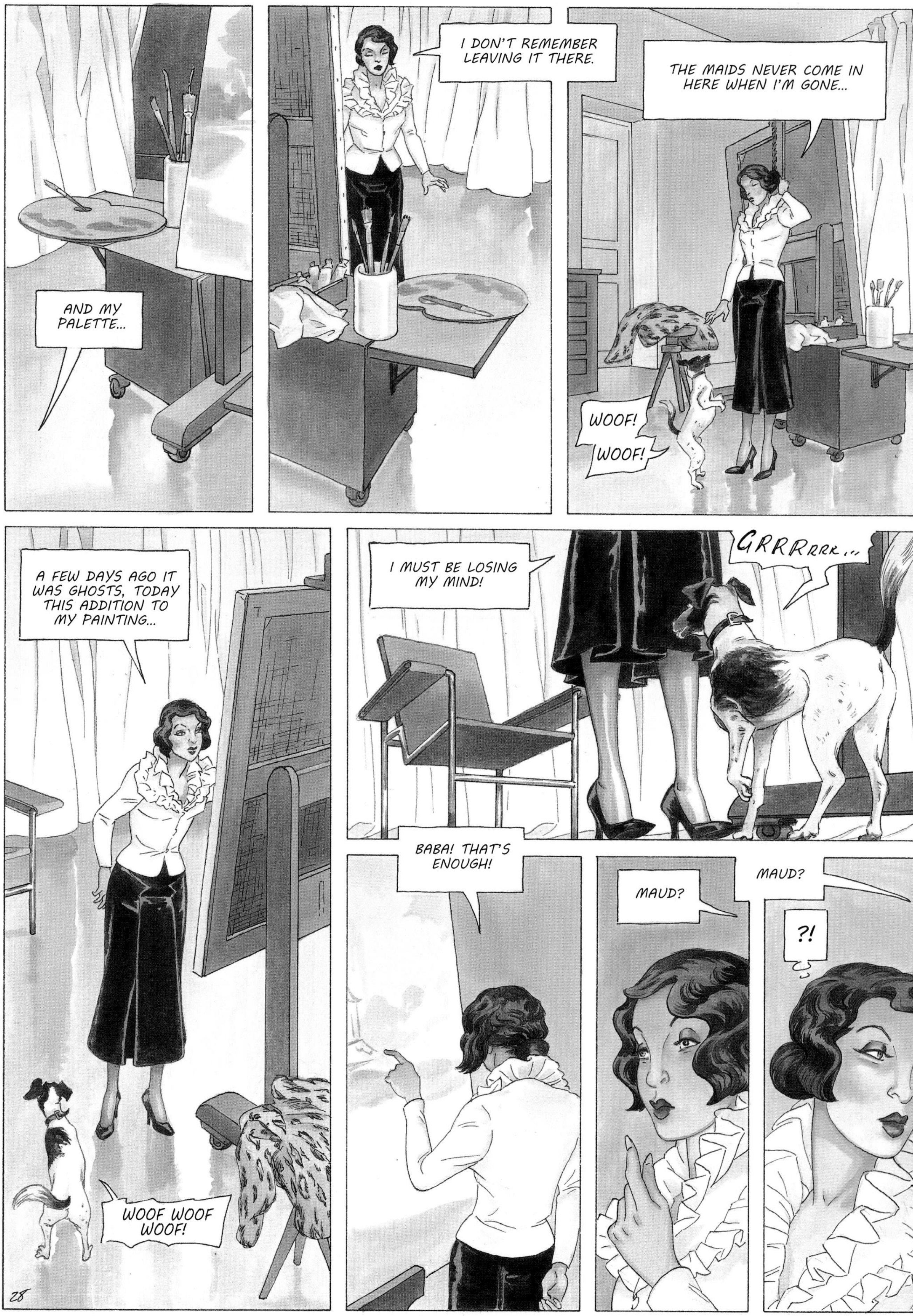
AND MY PALETTE...
I DON'T REMEMBER LEAVING IT THERE.
THE MAIDS NEVER COME IN HERE WHEN I'M GONE...
WOOF!
WOOF!
A FEW DAYS AGO IT WAS GHOSTS, TODAY THIS ADDITION TO MY PAINTING...
WOOF WOOF WOOF!
28
I MUST BE LOSING MY MIND!
GRRRrrr...
BABA! THAT'S ENOUGH!
MAUD?
MAUD?
?!

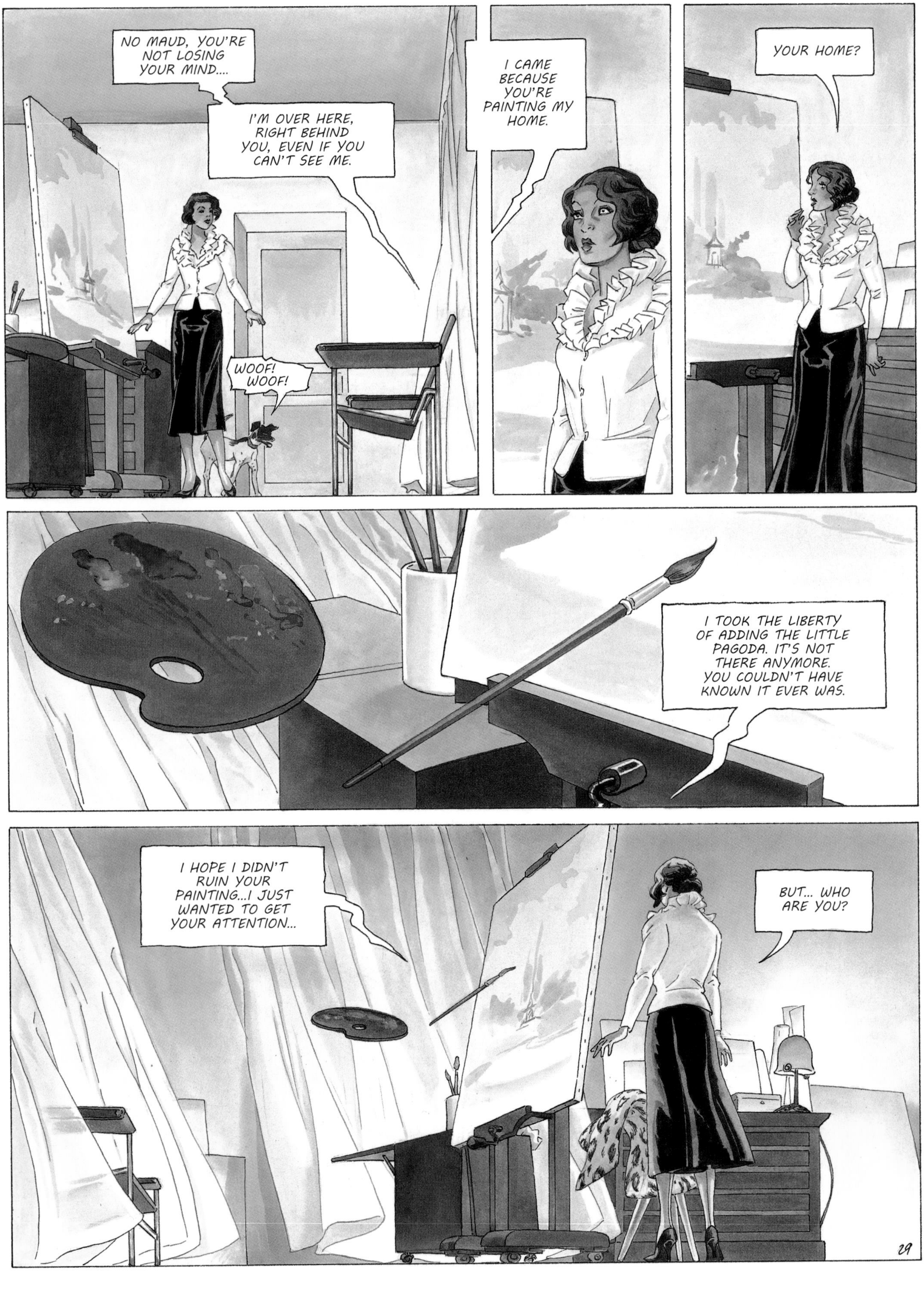
NO MAUD, YOU'RE NOT LOSING YOUR MIND....
I'M OVER HERE, RIGHT BEHIND YOU, EVEN IF YOU CAN'T SEE ME.
WOOF! WOOF!
I CAME BECAUSE YOU'RE PAINTING MY HOME.
YOUR HOME?
I TOOK THE LIBERTY OF ADDING THE LITTLE PAGODA. IT'S NOT THERE ANYMORE. YOU COULDN'T HAVE KNOWN IT EVER WAS.
I HOPE I DIDN'T RUIN YOUR PAINTING...I JUST WANTED TO GET YOUR ATTENTION...
BUT... WHO ARE YOU?
29

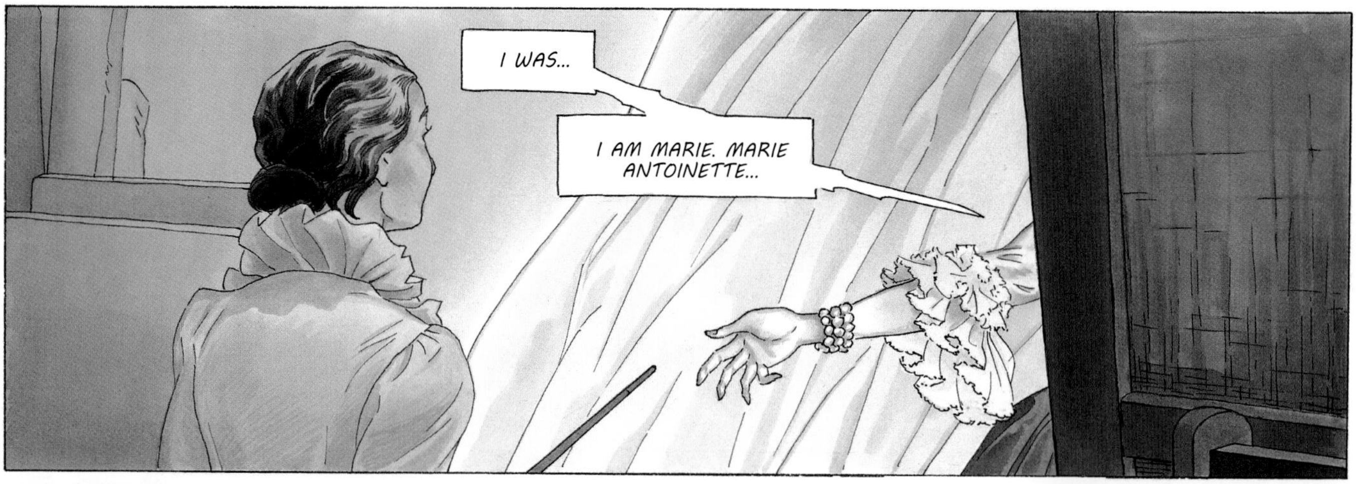
I WAS...
I AM MARIE. MARIE ANTOINETTE...

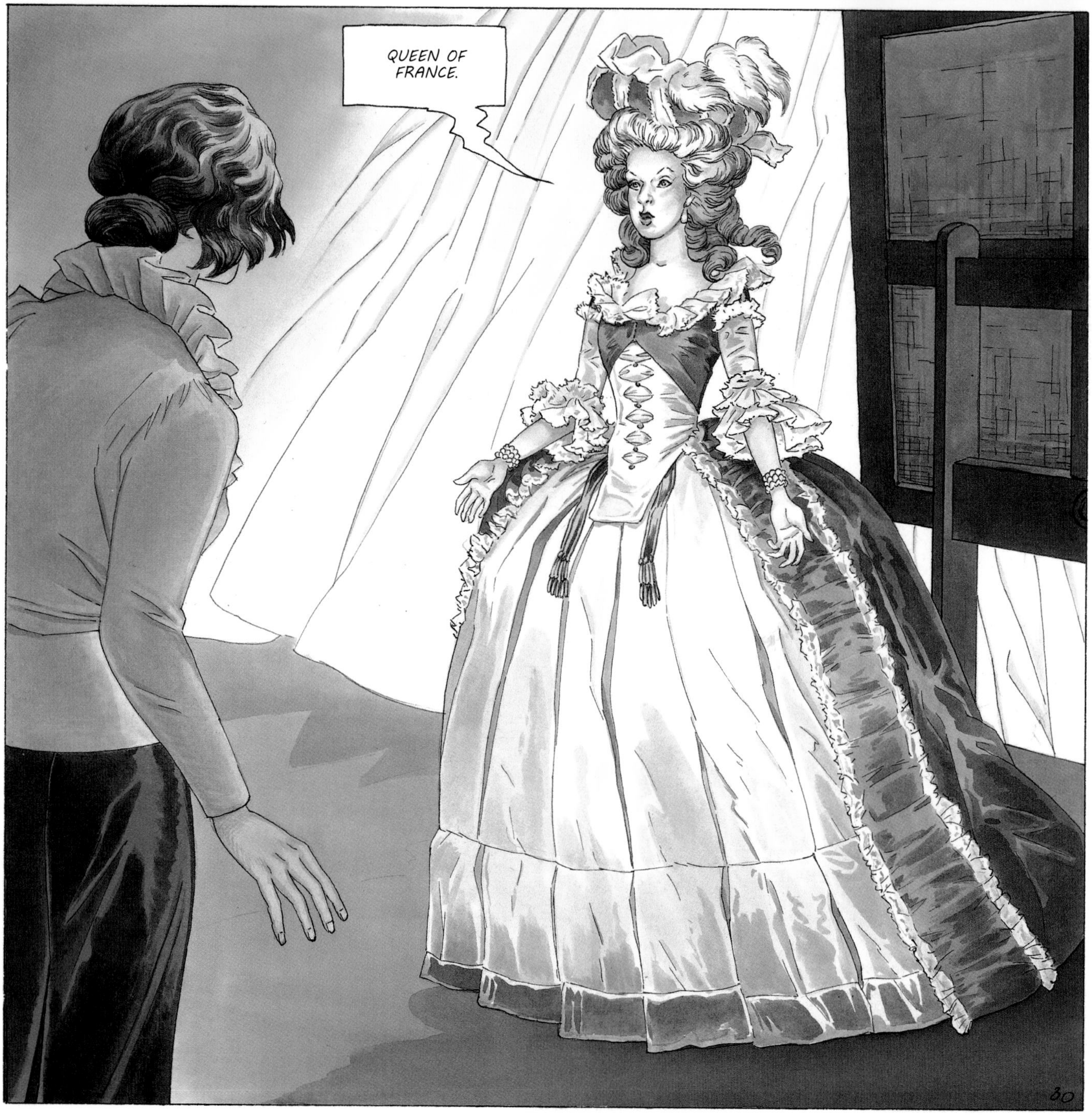
QUEEN OF FRANCE.

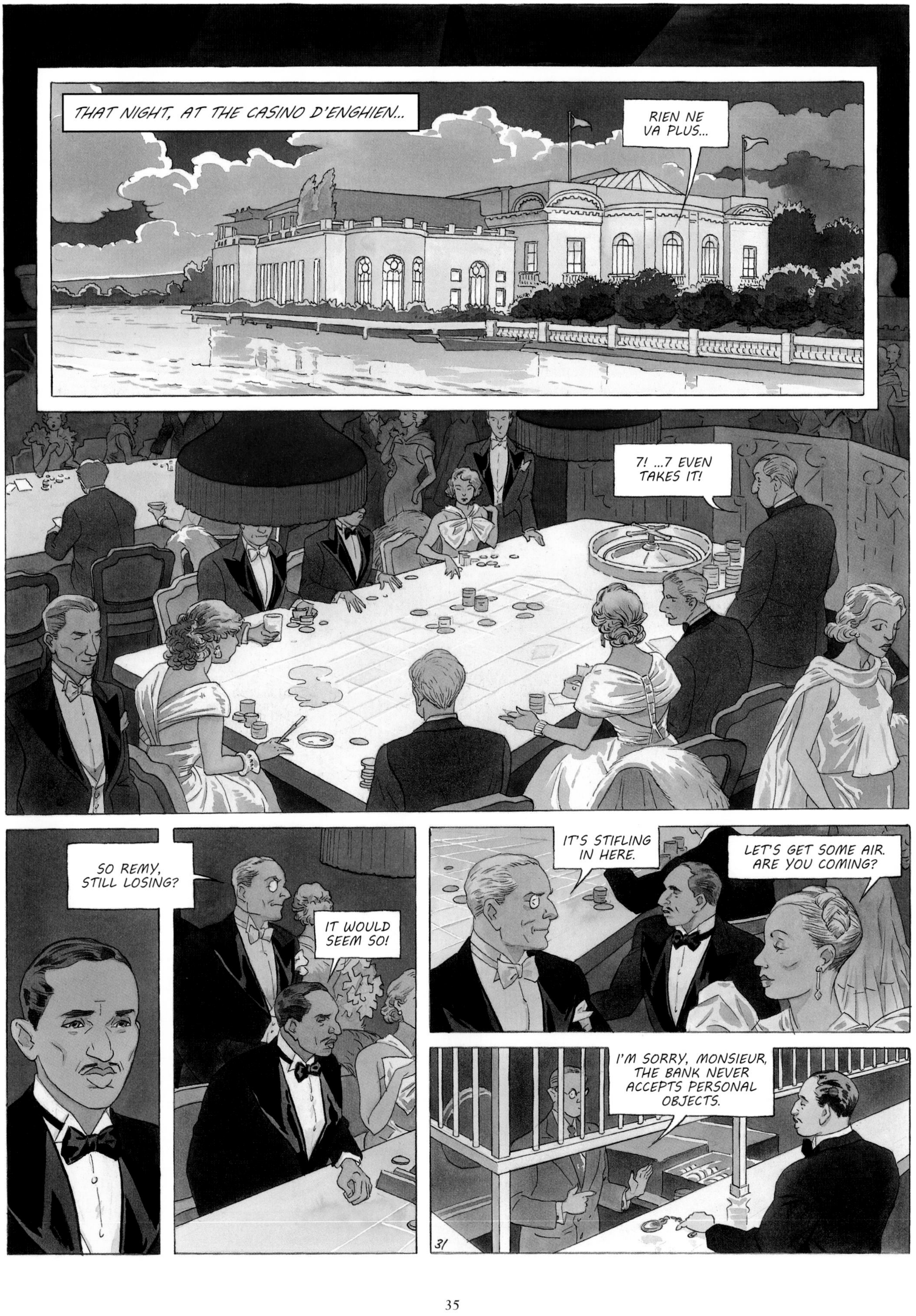
THAT NIGHT, AT THE CASINO D'ENGHIEN...
RIEN NE VA PLUS...
7! ...7 EVEN TAKES IT!
SO REMY, STILL LOSING?
IT WOULD SEEM SO!
IT'S STIFLING IN HERE.
LET'S GET SOME AIR. ARE YOU COMING?
I'M SORRY, MONSIEUR, THE BANK NEVER ACCEPTS PERSONAL OBJECTS.

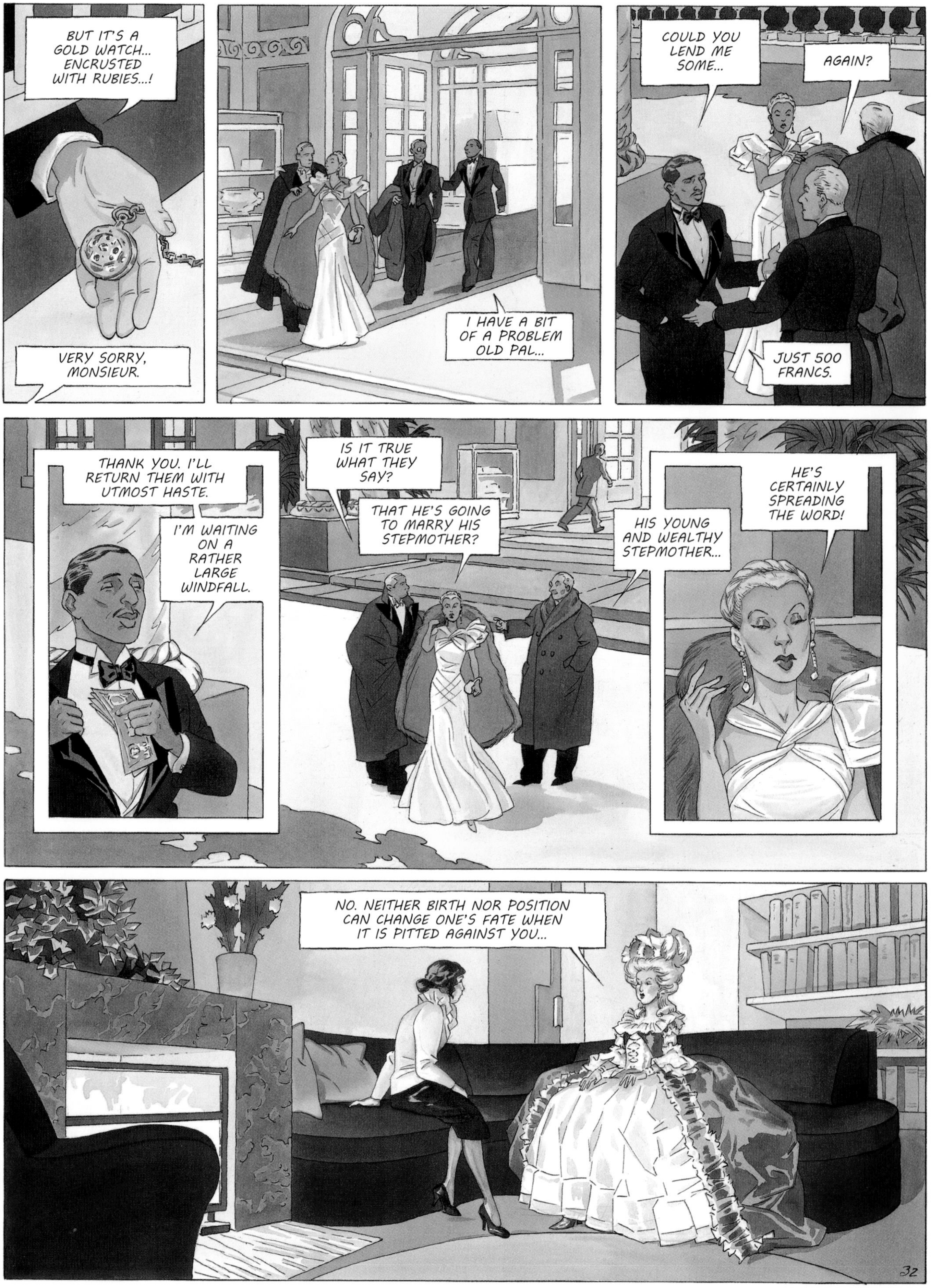

BUT IT'S A GOLD WATCH... ENCRUSTED WITH RUBIES...!
VERY SORRY, MONSIEUR.
I HAVE A BIT OF A PROBLEM OLD PAL...
COULD YOU LEND ME SOME...
AGAIN?
JUST 500 FRANCS.
THANK YOU. I'LL RETURN THEM WITH UTMOST HASTE.
I'M WAITING ON A RATHER LARGE WINDFALL.
IS IT TRUE WHAT THEY SAY?
THAT HE'S GOING TO MARRY HIS STEPMOTHER?
HIS YOUNG AND WEALTHY STEPMOTHER...
HE'S CERTAINLY SPREADING THE WORD!
NO. NEITHER BIRTH NOR POSITION CAN CHANGE ONE'S FATE WHEN IT IS PITTED AGAINST YOU...
32

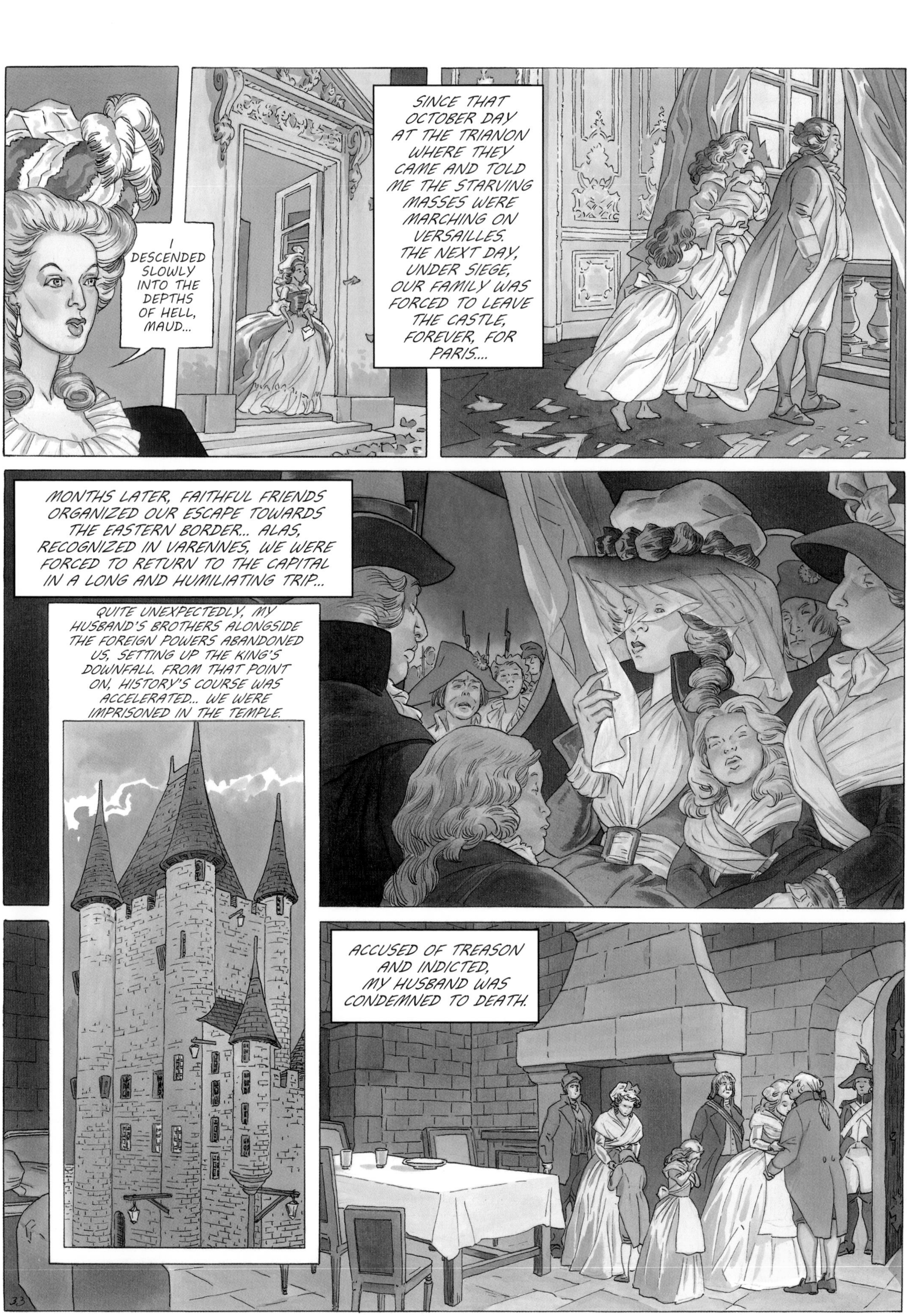
I DESCENDED SLOWLY INTO THE DEPTHS OF HELL, MAUD...
SINCE THAT OCTOBER DAY AT THE TRIANON WHERE THEY CAME AND TOLD ME THE STARVING MASSES WERE MARCHING ON VERSAILLES. THE NEXT DAY, UNDER SIEGE, OUR FAMILY WAS FORCED TO LEAVE THE CASTLE, FOREVER, FOR PARIS...
MONTHS LATER, FAITHFUL FRIENDS ORGANIZED OUR ESCAPE TOWARDS THE EASTERN BORDER... ALAS, RECOGNIZED IN VARENNES, WE WERE FORCED TO RETURN TO THE CAPITAL IN A LONG AND HUMILIATING TRIP...
QUITE UNEXPECTEDLY, MY HUSBAND'S BROTHERS ALONGSIDE THE FOREIGN POWERS ABANDONED US, SETTING UP THE KING'S DOWNFALL. FROM THAT POINT ON, HISTORY'S COURSE WAS ACCELERATED... WE WERE IMPRISONED IN THE TEMPLE.
ACCUSED OF TREASON AND INDICTED, MY HUSBAND WAS CONDEMNED TO DEATH.
33

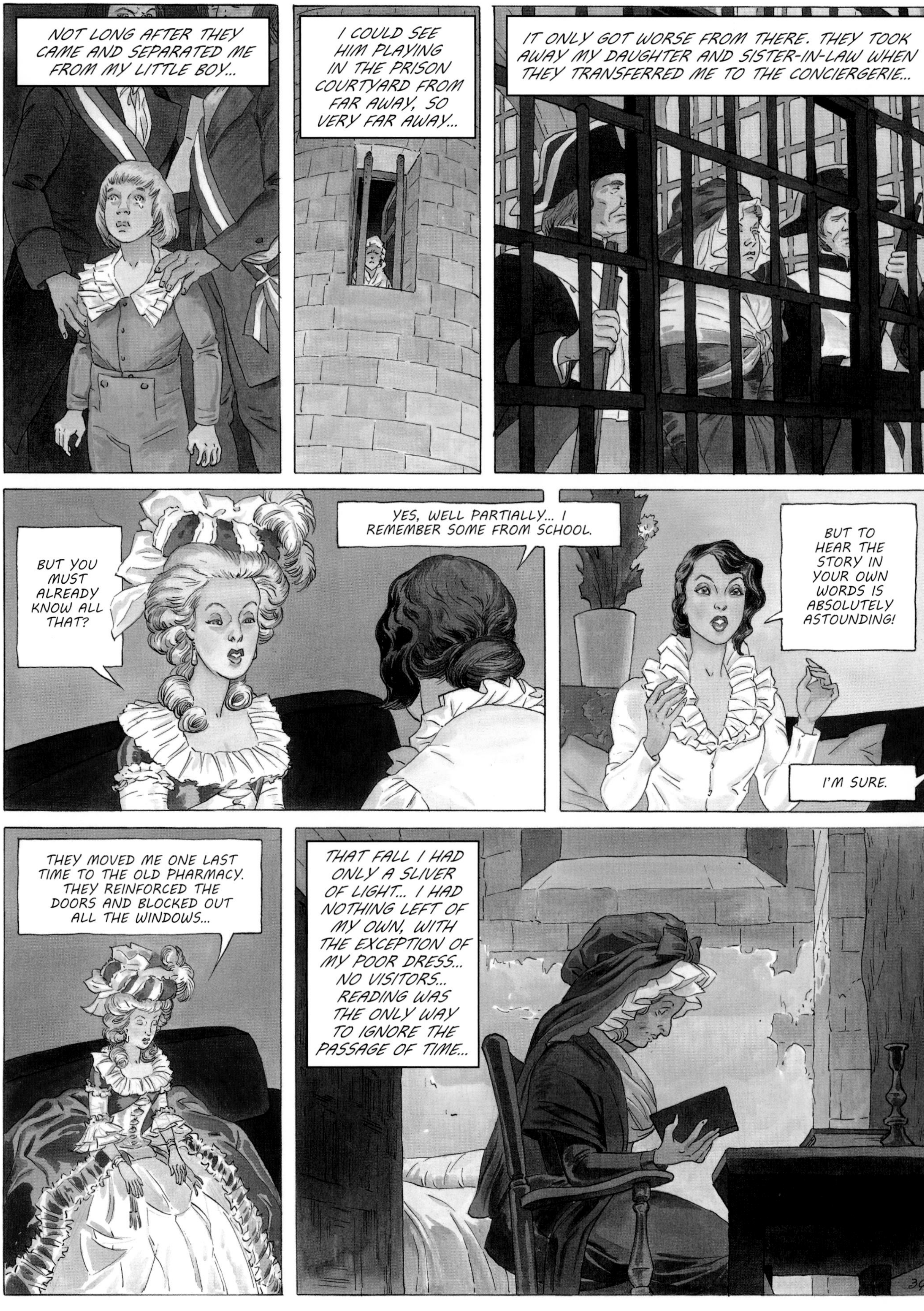
NOT LONG AFTER THEY CAME AND SEPARATED ME FROM MY LITTLE BOY...
I COULD SEE HIM PLAYING IN THE PRISON COURTYARD FROM FAR AWAY, SO VERY FAR AWAY...
IT ONLY GOT WORSE FROM THERE. THEY TOOK AWAY MY DAUGHTER AND SISTER-IN-LAW WHEN THEY TRANSFERRED ME TO THE CONCIERGERIE...
BUT YOU MUST ALREADY KNOW ALL THAT?
YES, WELL PARTIALLY... I REMEMBER SOME FROM SCHOOL.
BUT TO HEAR THE STORY IN YOUR OWN WORDS IS ABSOLUTELY ASTOUNDING!
I'M SURE.
THEY MOVED ME ONE LAST TIME TO THE OLD PHARMACY. THEY REINFORCED THE DOORS AND BLOCKED OUT ALL THE WINDOWS...
THAT FALL I HAD ONLY A SLIVER OF LIGHT... I HAD NOTHING LEFT OF MY OWN, WITH THE EXCEPTION OF MY POOR DRESS... NO VISITORS... READING WAS THE ONLY WAY TO IGNORE THE PASSAGE OF TIME...

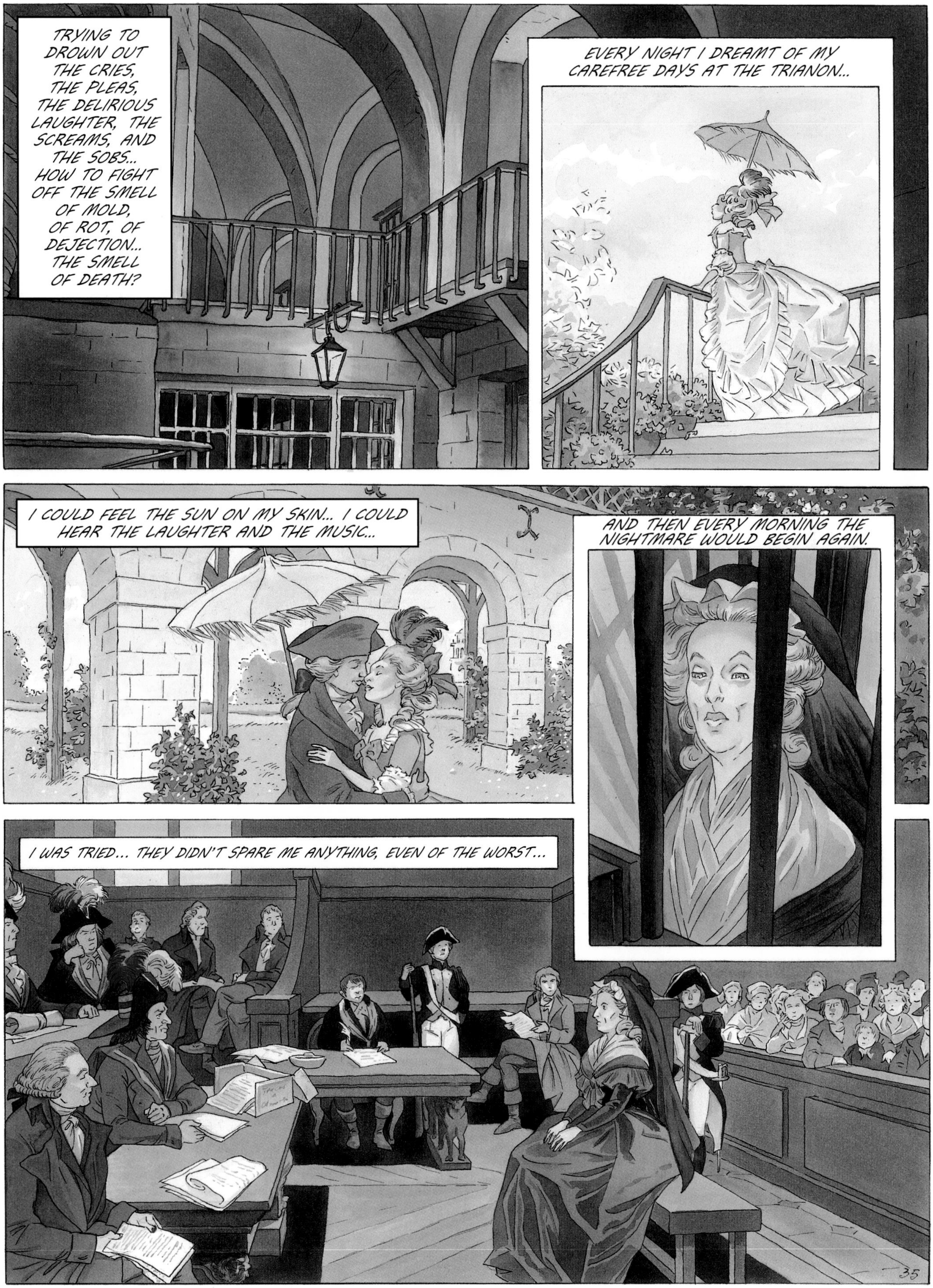
TRYING TO DROWN OUT THE CRIES, THE PLEAS, THE DELIRIOUS LAUGHTER, THE SCREAMS, AND THE SOBS... HOW TO FIGHT OFF THE SMELL OF MOLD, OF ROT, OF DEJECTION... THE SMELL OF DEATH?
EVERY NIGHT I DREAMT OF MY CAREFREE DAYS AT THE TRIANON...
I COULD FEEL THE SUN ON MY SKIN... I COULD HEAR THE LAUGHTER AND THE MUSIC...
AND THEN EVERY MORNING THE NIGHTMARE WOULD BEGIN AGAIN.
I WAS TRIED... THEY DIDN'T SPARE ME ANYTHING, EVEN OF THE WORST...

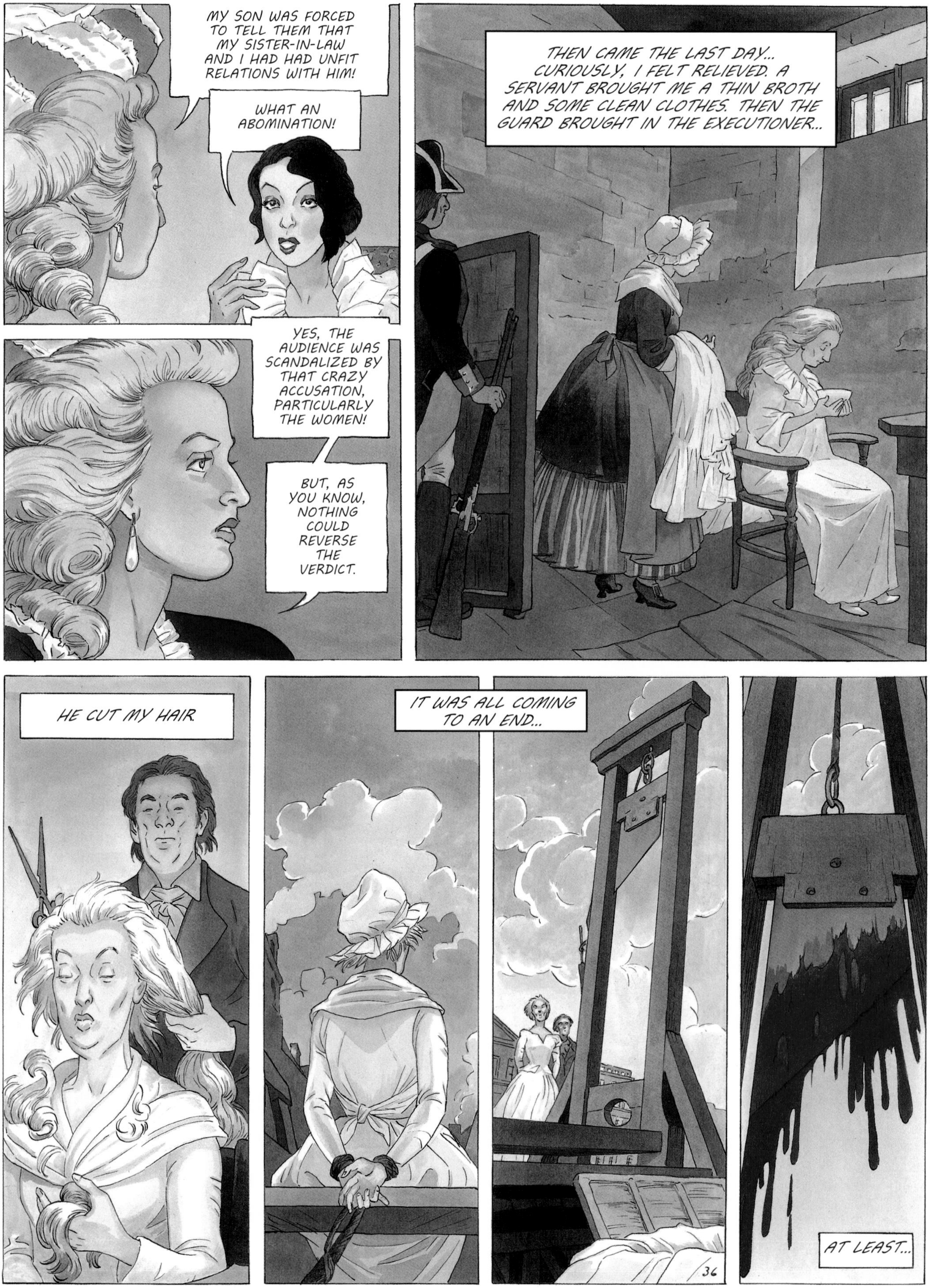
MY SON WAS FORCED TO TELL THEM THAT MY SISTER-IN-LAW AND I HAD HAD UNFIT RELATIONS WITH HIM!
WHAT AN ABOMINATION!
THEN CAME THE LAST DAY... CURIOUSLY, I FELT RELIEVED. A SERVANT BROUGHT ME A THIN BROTH AND SOME CLEAN CLOTHES. THEN THE GUARD BROUGHT IN THE EXECUTIONER...
YES, THE AUDIENCE WAS SCANDALIZED BY THAT CRAZY ACCUSATION, PARTICULARLY THE WOMEN!
BUT, AS YOU KNOW, NOTHING COULD REVERSE THE VERDICT.
HE CUT MY HAIR.
IT WAS ALL COMING TO AN END...
AT LEAST...
36

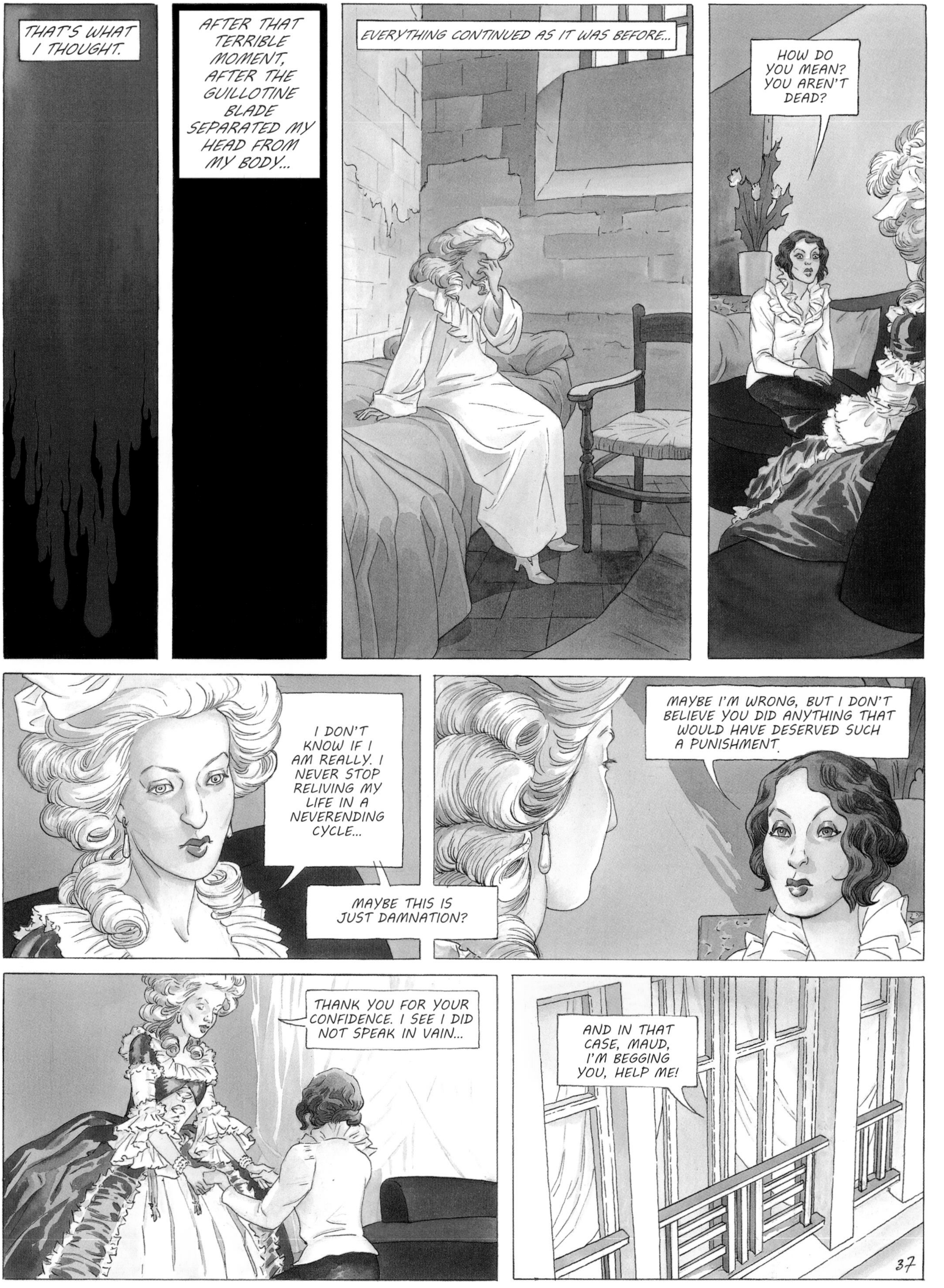

THAT'S WHAT I THOUGHT.
AFTER THAT TERRIBLE MOMENT, AFTER THE GUILLOTINE BLADE SEPARATED MY HEAD FROM MY BODY...
EVERYTHING CONTINUED AS IT WAS BEFORE...
HOW DO YOU MEAN? YOU AREN'T DEAD?
I DON'T KNOW IF I AM REALLY. I NEVER STOP RELIVING MY LIFE IN A NEVERENDING CYCLE...
MAYBE THIS IS JUST DAMNATION?
MAYBE I'M WRONG, BUT I DON'T BELIEVE YOU DID ANYTHING THAT WOULD HAVE DESERVED SUCH A PUNISHMENT.
THANK YOU FOR YOUR CONFIDENCE. I SEE I DID NOT SPEAK IN VAIN...
AND IN THAT CASE, MAUD, I'M BEGGING YOU, HELP ME!
37

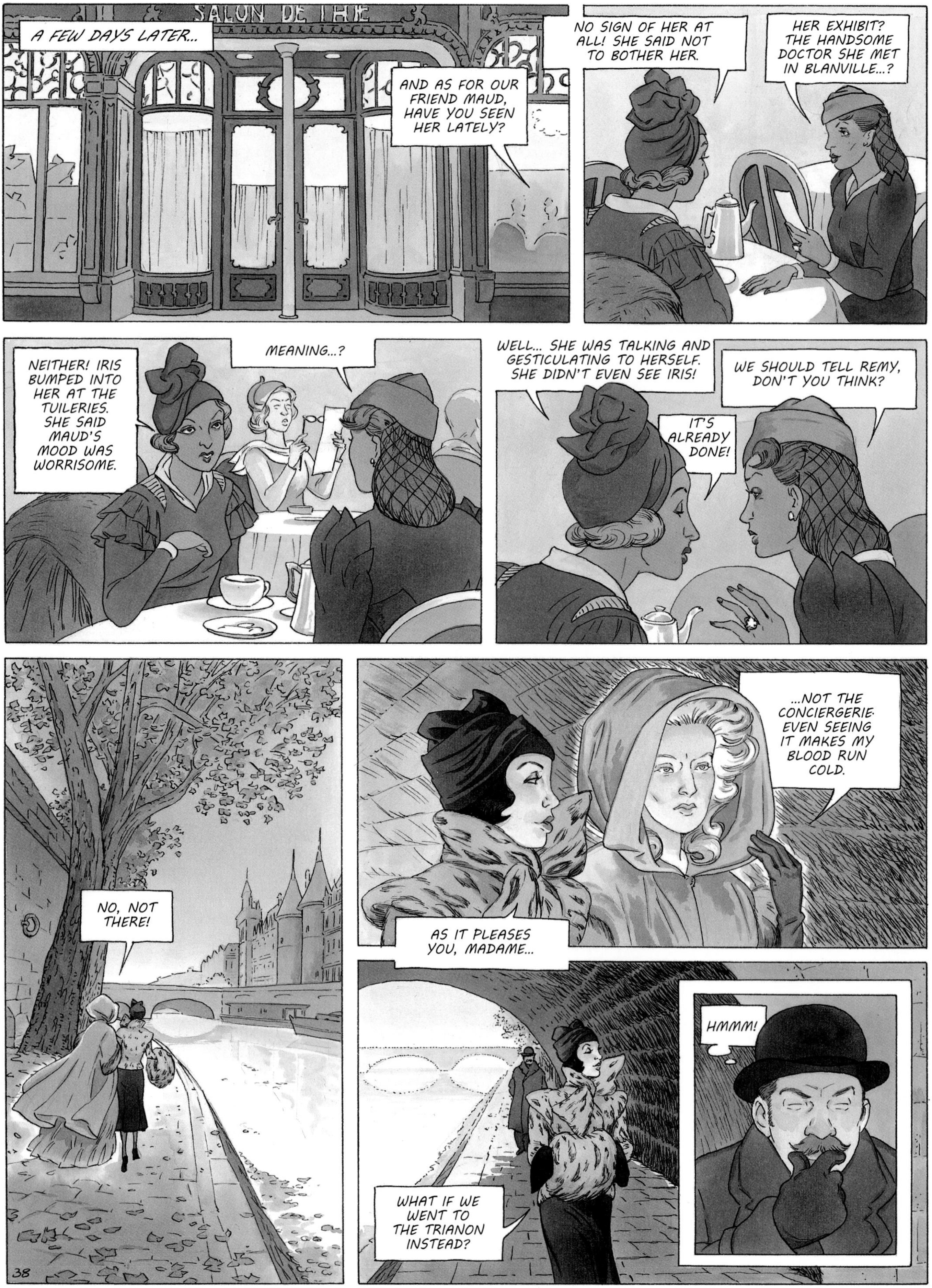
SALON DE THE
A FEW DAYS LATER...
AND AS FOR OUR FRIEND MAUD, HAVE YOU SEEN HER LATELY?
NO SIGN OF HER AT ALL! SHE SAID NOT TO BOTHER HER.
HER EXHIBIT? THE HANDSOME DOCTOR SHE MET IN BLANVILLE...?
NEITHER! IRIS BUMPED INTO HER AT THE TUILERIES. SHE SAID MAUD'S MOOD WAS WORRISOME.
MEANING...?
WELL... SHE WAS TALKING AND GESTICULATING TO HERSELF. SHE DIDN'T EVEN SEE IRIS!
WE SHOULD TELL REMY, DON'T YOU THINK?
IT'S ALREADY DONE!
NO, NOT THERE!
...NOT THE CONCIERGERIE. EVEN SEEING IT MAKES MY BLOOD RUN COLD.
AS IT PLEASES YOU, MADAME...
WHAT IF WE WENT TO THE TRIANON INSTEAD?
HMMM!
38

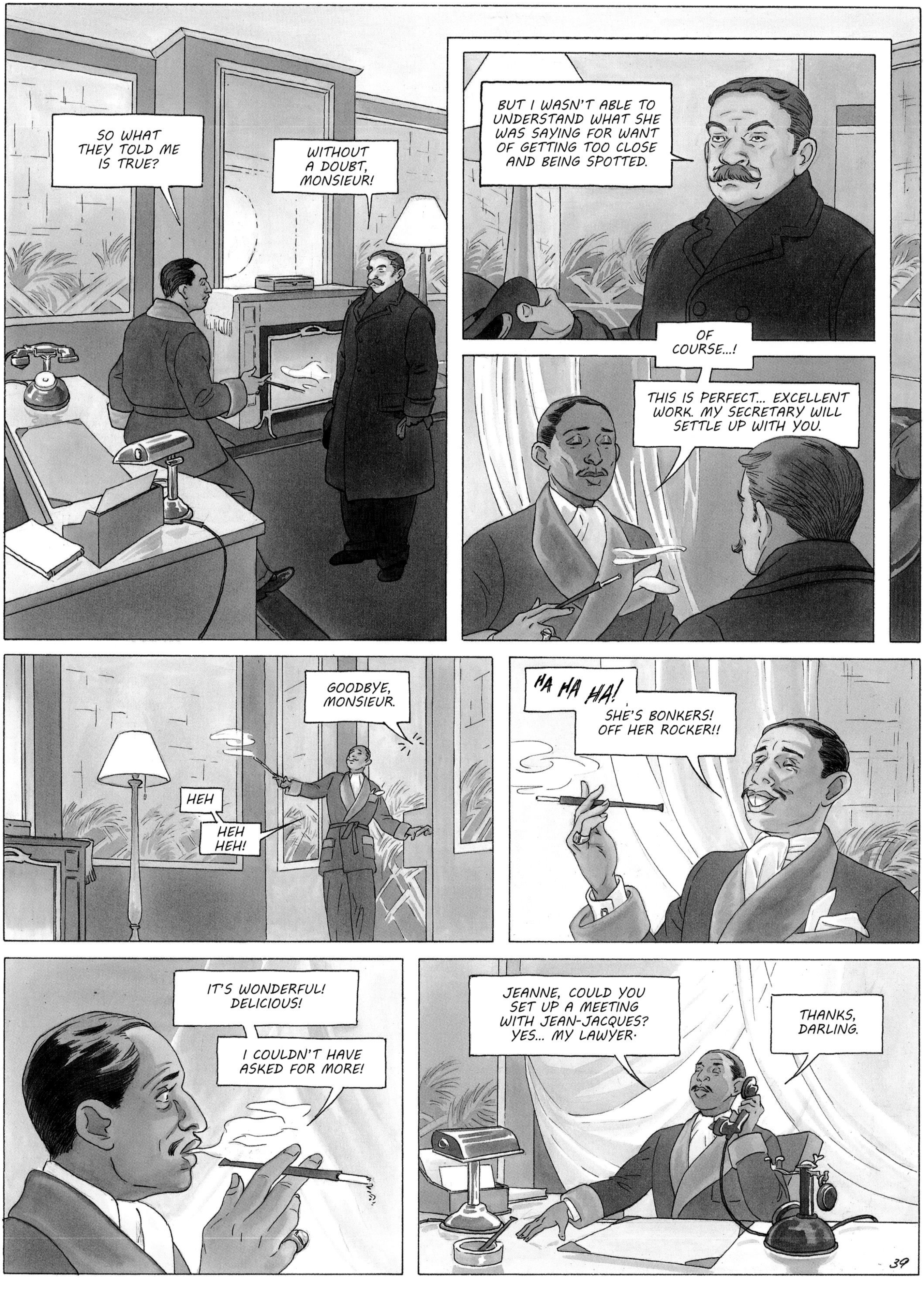
SO WHAT THEY TOLD ME IS TRUE?
WITHOUT A DOUBT, MONSIEUR!
BUT I WASN'T ABLE TO UNDERSTAND WHAT SHE WAS SAYING FOR WANT OF GETTING TOO CLOSE AND BEING SPOTTED.
OF COURSE...!
THIS IS PERFECT... EXCELLENT WORK. MY SECRETARY WILL SETTLE UP WITH YOU.
GOODBYE, MONSIEUR.
HEH
HEH HEH!
HA HA HA!
SHE'S BONKERS! OFF HER ROCKER!!
IT'S WONDERFUL! DELICIOUS!
I COULDN'T HAVE ASKED FOR MORE!
JEANNE, COULD YOU SET UP A MEETING WITH JEAN-JACQUES? YES... MY LAWYER.
THANKS, DARLING.
39

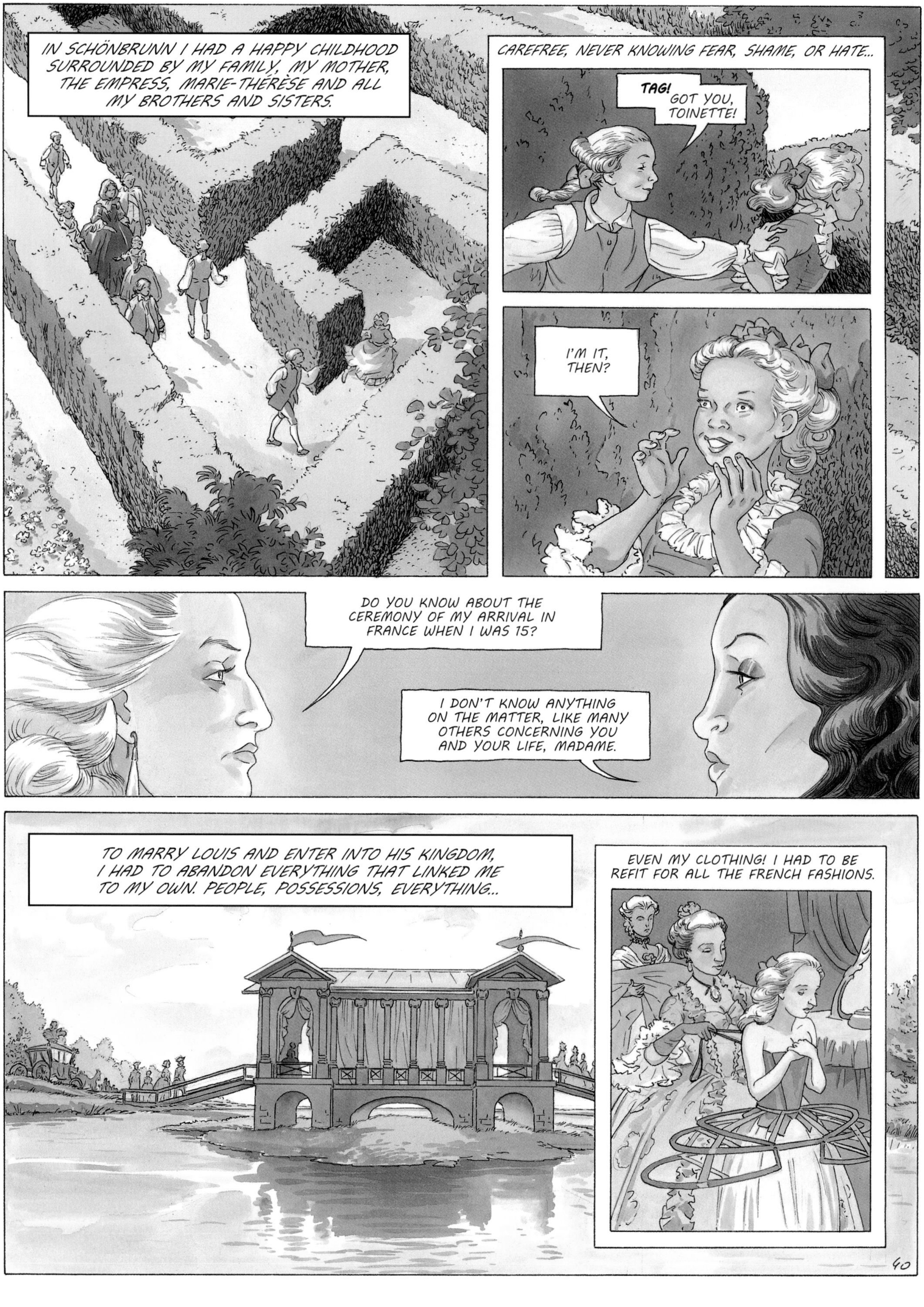

IN SCHÖNBRUNN I HAD A HAPPY CHILDHOOD SURROUNDED BY MY FAMILY, MY MOTHER, THE EMPRESS, MARIE-THÉRÈSE AND ALL MY BROTHERS AND SISTERS.
CAREFREE, NEVER KNOWING FEAR, SHAME, OR HATE...
TAG! GOT YOU, TOINETTE!
I'M IT, THEN?
DO YOU KNOW ABOUT THE CEREMONY OF MY ARRIVAL IN FRANCE WHEN I WAS 15?
I DON'T KNOW ANYTHING ON THE MATTER, LIKE MANY OTHERS CONCERNING YOU AND YOUR LIFE, MADAME.
TO MARRY LOUIS AND ENTER INTO HIS KINGDOM, I HAD TO ABANDON EVERYTHING THAT LINKED ME TO MY OWN. PEOPLE, POSSESSIONS, EVERYTHING...
EVEN MY CLOTHING! I HAD TO BE REFIT FOR ALL THE FRENCH FASHIONS.
40

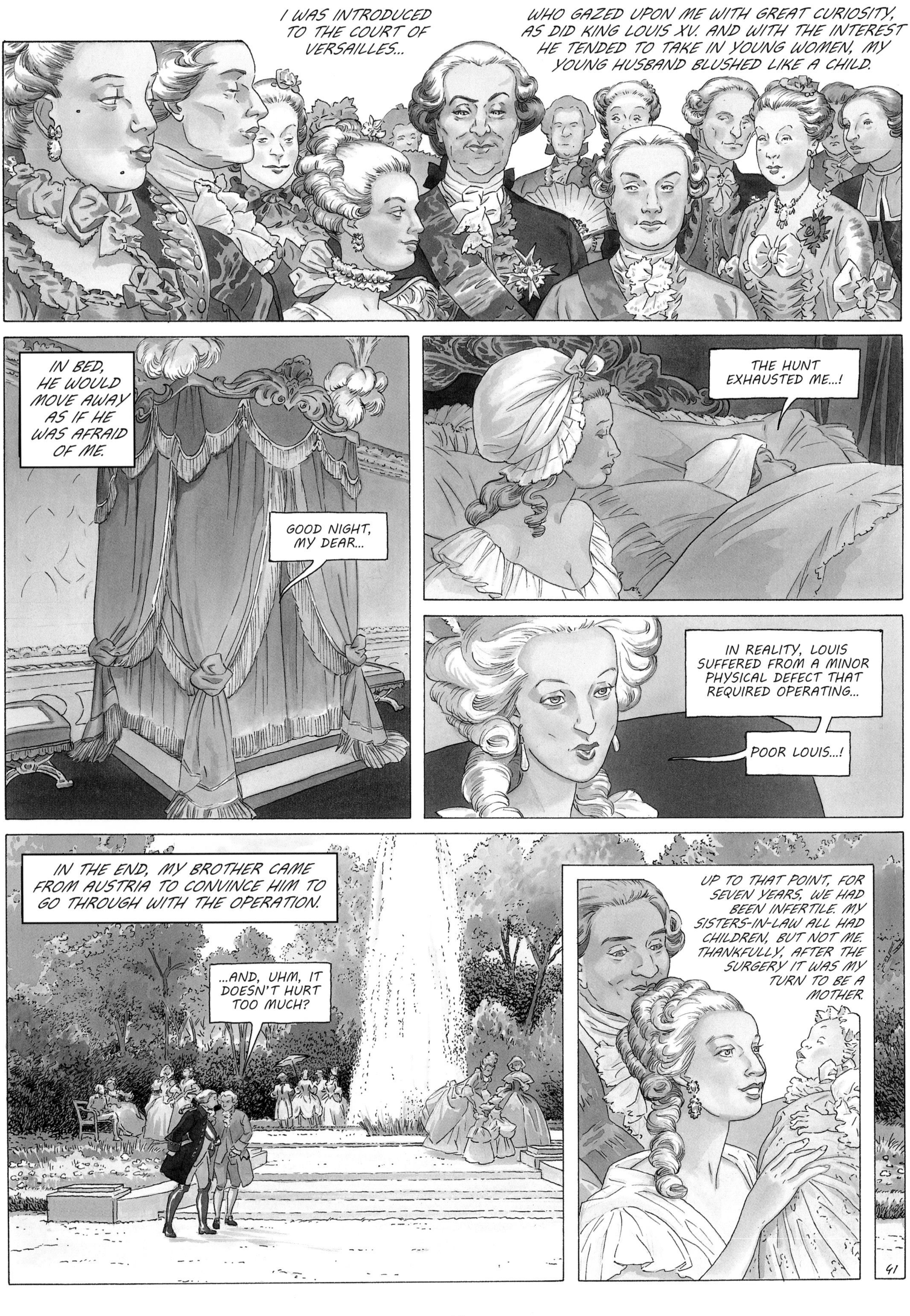
I WAS INTRODUCED TO THE COURT OF VERSAILLES...
WHO GAZED UPON ME WITH GREAT CURIOSITY, AS DID KING LOUIS XV. AND WITH THE INTEREST HE TENDED TO TAKE IN YOUNG WOMEN, MY YOUNG HUSBAND BLUSHED LIKE A CHILD.
IN BED, HE WOULD MOVE AWAY AS IF HE WAS AFRAID OF ME.
GOOD NIGHT, MY DEAR...
THE HUNT EXHAUSTED ME...!
IN REALITY, LOUIS SUFFERED FROM A MINOR PHYSICAL DEFECT THAT REQUIRED OPERATING...
POOR LOUIS...!
IN THE END, MY BROTHER CAME FROM AUSTRIA TO CONVINCE HIM TO GO THROUGH WITH THE OPERATION.
...AND, UHM, IT DOESN'T HURT TOO MUCH?
UP TO THAT POINT, FOR SEVEN YEARS, WE HAD BEEN INFERTILE. MY SISTERS-IN-LAW ALL HAD CHILDREN, BUT NOT ME. THANKFULLY, AFTER THE SURGERY IT WAS MY TURN TO BE A MOTHER.
41

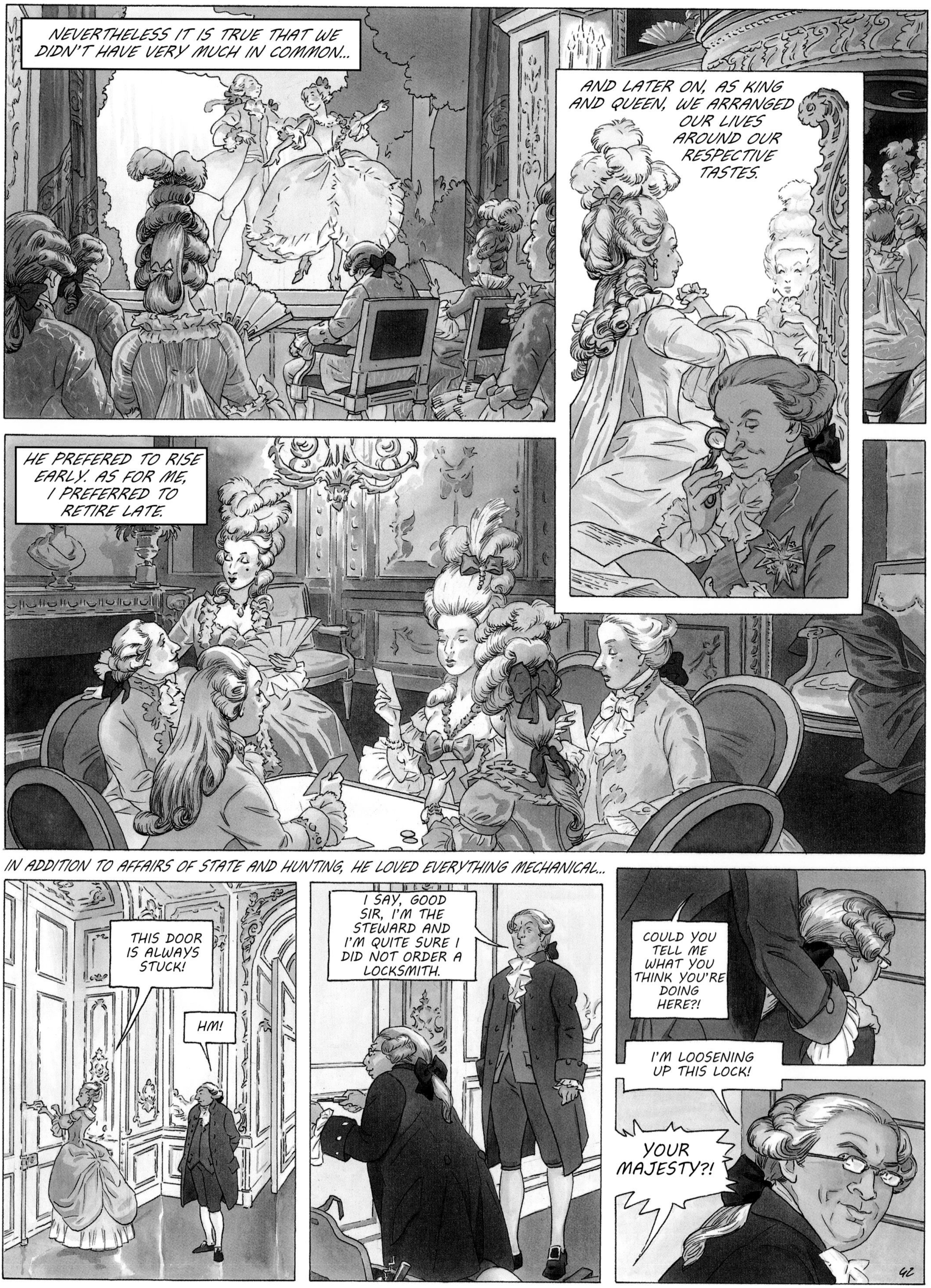
NEVERTHELESS IT IS TRUE THAT WE DIDN'T HAVE VERY MUCH IN COMMON...
AND LATER ON, AS KING AND QUEEN, WE ARRANGED OUR LIVES AROUND OUR RESPECTIVE TASTES.
HE PREFERED TO RISE EARLY. AS FOR ME, I PREFERRED TO RETIRE LATE.
IN ADDITION TO AFFAIRS OF STATE AND HUNTING, HE LOVED EVERYTHING MECHANICAL...
THIS DOOR IS ALWAYS STUCK!
HM!
I SAY, GOOD SIR, I'M THE STEWARD AND I'M QUITE SURE I DID NOT ORDER A LOCKSMITH.
COULD YOU TELL ME WHAT YOU THINK YOU'RE DOING HERE?!
I'M LOOSENING UP THIS LOCK!
YOUR MAJESTY?!

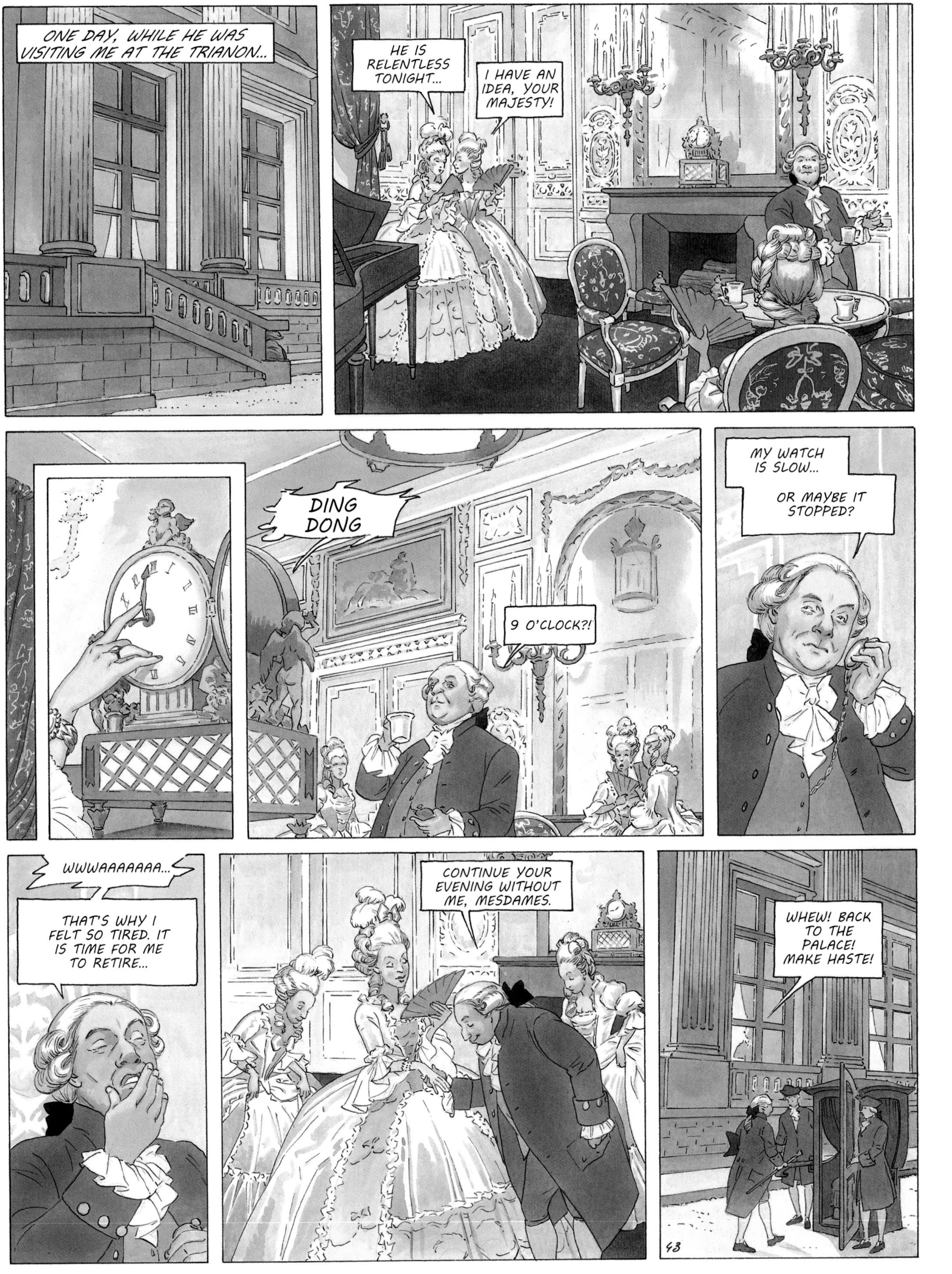
ONE DAY, WHILE HE WAS VISITING ME AT THE TRIANON...
HE IS RELENTLESS TONIGHT...
I HAVE AN IDEA, YOUR MAJESTY!
DING DONG
9 O'CLOCK?!
MY WATCH IS SLOW...
OR MAYBE IT STOPPED?
WWWAAAAAAA...
THAT'S WHY I FELT SO TIRED. IT IS TIME FOR ME TO RETIRE...
CONTINUE YOUR EVENING WITHOUT ME, MESDAMES.
WHEW! BACK TO THE PALACE! MAKE HASTE!
48

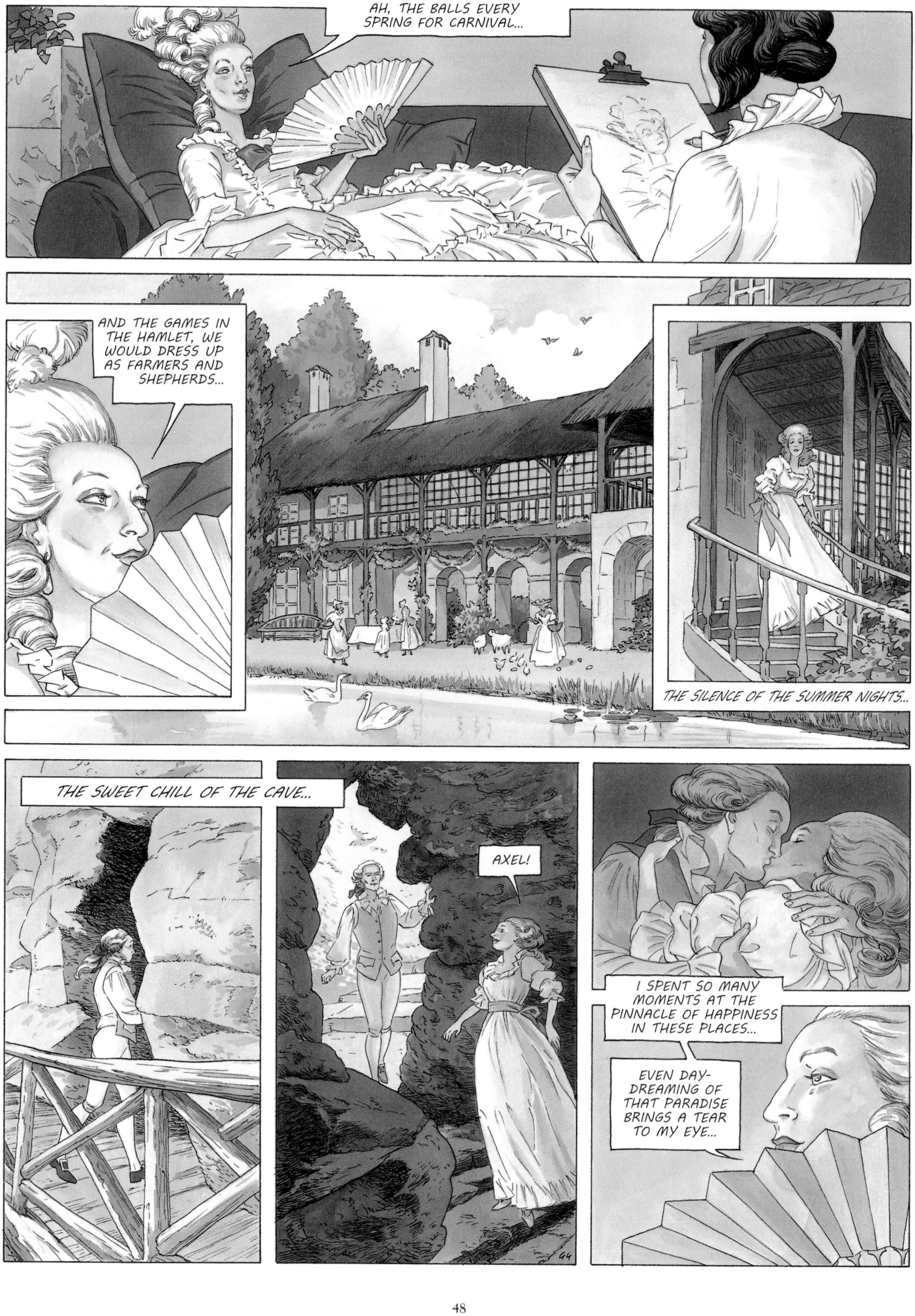
AH, THE BALLS EVERY SPRING FOR CARNIVAL...
AND THE GAMES IN THE HAMLET, WE WOULD DRESS UP AS FARMERS AND SHEPHERDS...
THE SILENCE OF THE SUMMER NIGHTS...
THE SWEET CHILL OF THE CAVE...
AXEL!
I SPENT SO MANY MOMENTS AT THE PINNACLE OF HAPPINESS IN THESE PLACES...
EVEN DAY-DREAMING OF THAT PARADISE BRINGS A TEAR TO MY EYE...

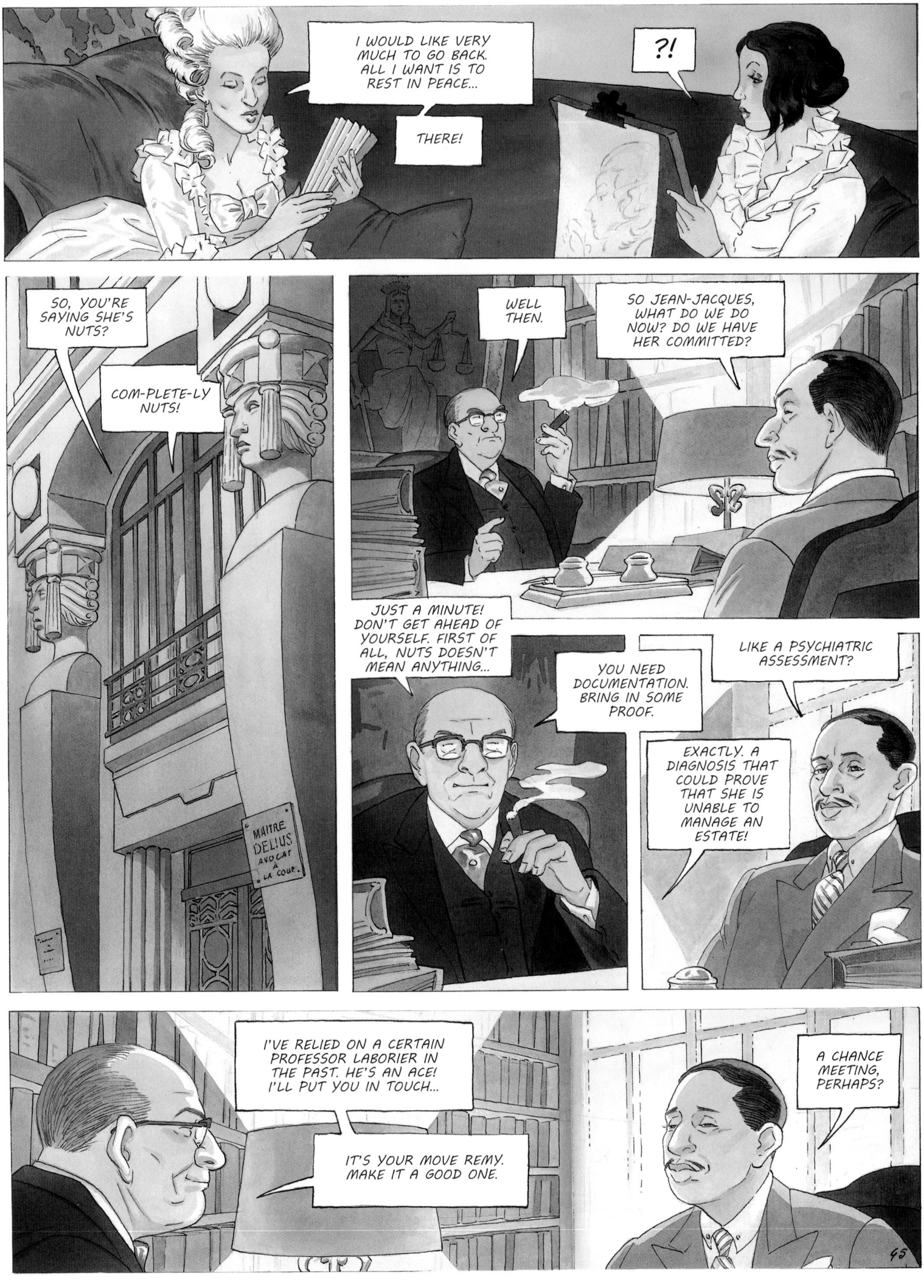
I WOULD LIKE VERY MUCH TO GO BACK. ALL I WANT IS TO REST IN PEACE...
THERE!
?!
SO, YOU'RE SAYING SHE'S NUTS?
COM-PLETE-LY NUTS!
MAITRE DELIUS AVOCAT À LA COUR
WELL THEN.
SO JEAN-JACQUES, WHAT DO WE DO NOW? DO WE HAVE HER COMMITTED?
JUST A MINUTE! DON'T GET AHEAD OF YOURSELF. FIRST OF ALL, NUTS DOESN'T MEAN ANYTHING...
YOU NEED DOCUMENTATION. BRING IN SOME PROOF.
LIKE A PSYCHIATRIC ASSESSMENT?
EXACTLY. A DIAGNOSIS THAT COULD PROVE THAT SHE IS UNABLE TO MANAGE AN ESTATE!
I'VE RELIED ON A CERTAIN PROFESSOR LABORIER IN THE PAST. HE'S AN ACE! I'LL PUT YOU IN TOUCH...
IT'S YOUR MOVE REMY. MAKE IT A GOOD ONE.
A CHANCE MEETING, PERHAPS?
45

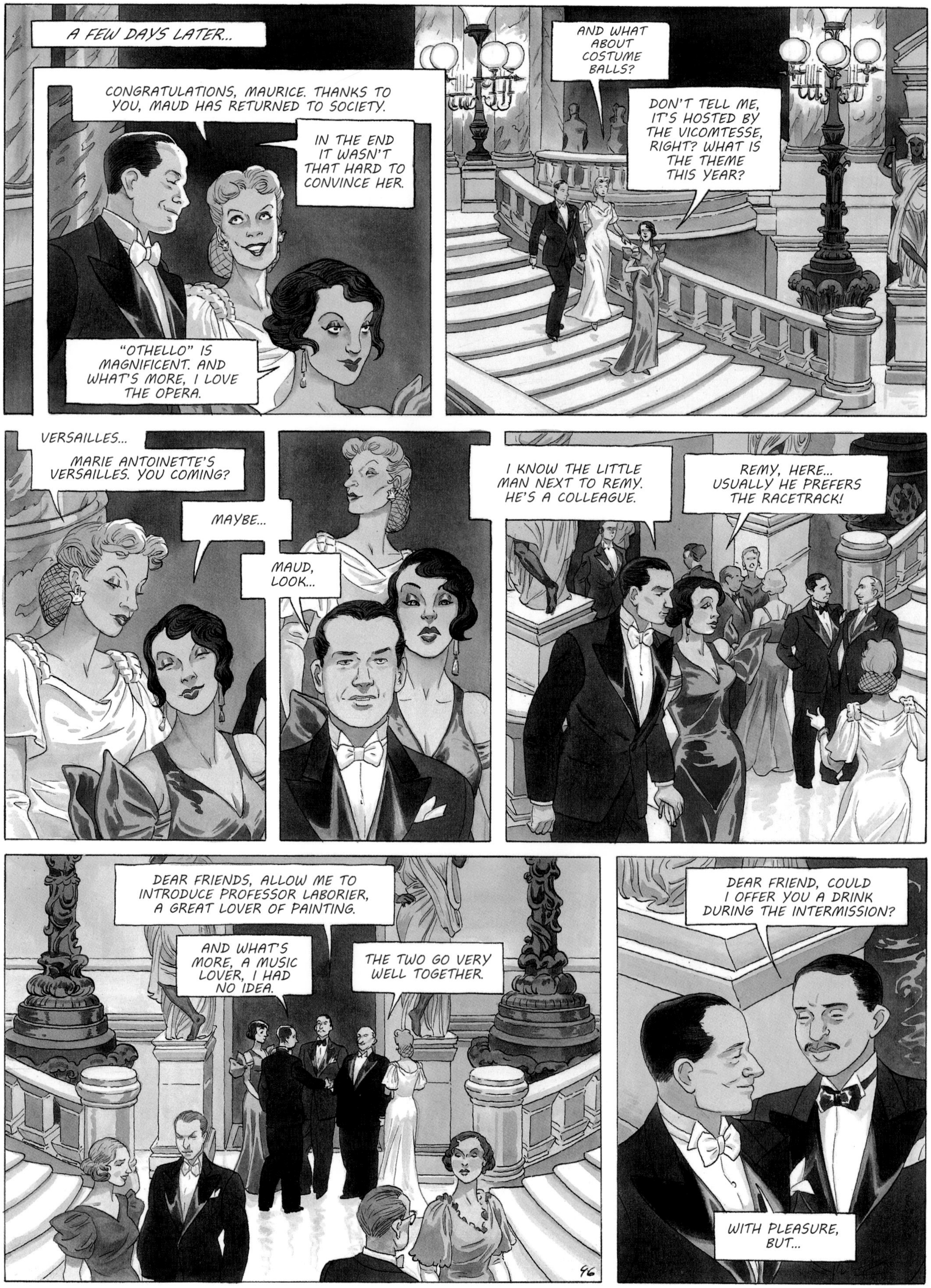
A FEW DAYS LATER...
CONGRATULATIONS, MAURICE. THANKS TO YOU, MAUD HAS RETURNED TO SOCIETY.
IN THE END IT WASN'T THAT HARD TO CONVINCE HER.
"OTHELLO" IS MAGNIFICENT. AND WHAT'S MORE, I LOVE THE OPERA.
AND WHAT ABOUT COSTUME BALLS?
DON'T TELL ME, IT'S HOSTED BY THE VICOMTESSE, RIGHT? WHAT IS THE THEME THIS YEAR?
VERSAILLES...
MARIE ANTOINETTE'S VERSAILLES. YOU COMING?
MAYBE...
MAUD, LOOK...
I KNOW THE LITTLE MAN NEXT TO REMY. HE'S A COLLEAGUE.
REMY, HERE... USUALLY HE PREFERS THE RACETRACK!
DEAR FRIENDS, ALLOW ME TO INTRODUCE PROFESSOR LABORIER, A GREAT LOVER OF PAINTING.
AND WHAT'S MORE, A MUSIC LOVER, I HAD NO IDEA.
THE TWO GO VERY WELL TOGETHER.
DEAR FRIEND, COULD I OFFER YOU A DRINK DURING THE INTERMISSION?
WITH PLEASURE, BUT...

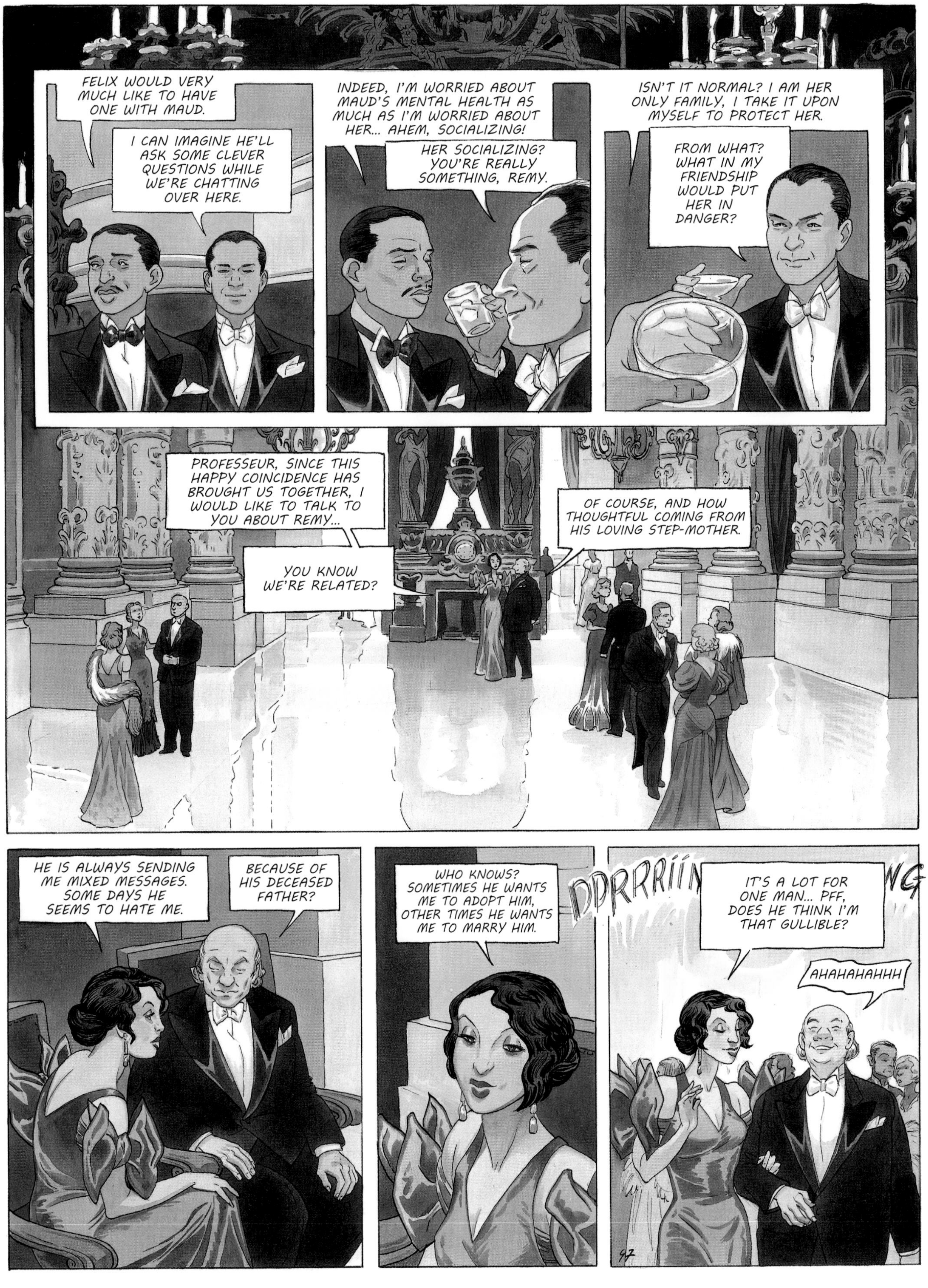
FELIX WOULD VERY MUCH LIKE TO HAVE ONE WITH MAUD.
I CAN IMAGINE HE'LL ASK SOME CLEVER QUESTIONS WHILE WE'RE CHATTING OVER HERE.
INDEED, I'M WORRIED ABOUT MAUD'S MENTAL HEALTH AS MUCH AS I'M WORRIED ABOUT HER... AHEM, SOCIALIZING!
HER SOCIALIZING? YOU'RE REALLY SOMETHING, REMY.
ISN'T IT NORMAL? I AM HER ONLY FAMILY, I TAKE IT UPON MYSELF TO PROTECT HER.
FROM WHAT? WHAT IN MY FRIENDSHIP WOULD PUT HER IN DANGER?
PROFESSEUR, SINCE THIS HAPPY COINCIDENCE HAS BROUGHT US TOGETHER, I WOULD LIKE TO TALK TO YOU ABOUT REMY...
YOU KNOW WE'RE RELATED?
OF COURSE, AND HOW THOUGHTFUL COMING FROM HIS LOVING STEP-MOTHER.
HE IS ALWAYS SENDING ME MIXED MESSAGES. SOME DAYS HE SEEMS TO HATE ME.
BECAUSE OF HIS DECEASED FATHER?
WHO KNOWS? SOMETIMES HE WANTS ME TO ADOPT HIM, OTHER TIMES HE WANTS ME TO MARRY HIM.
DDRRRIIING
IT'S A LOT FOR ONE MAN... PFF, DOES HE THINK I'M THAT GULLIBLE?
AHAHAHAHHH

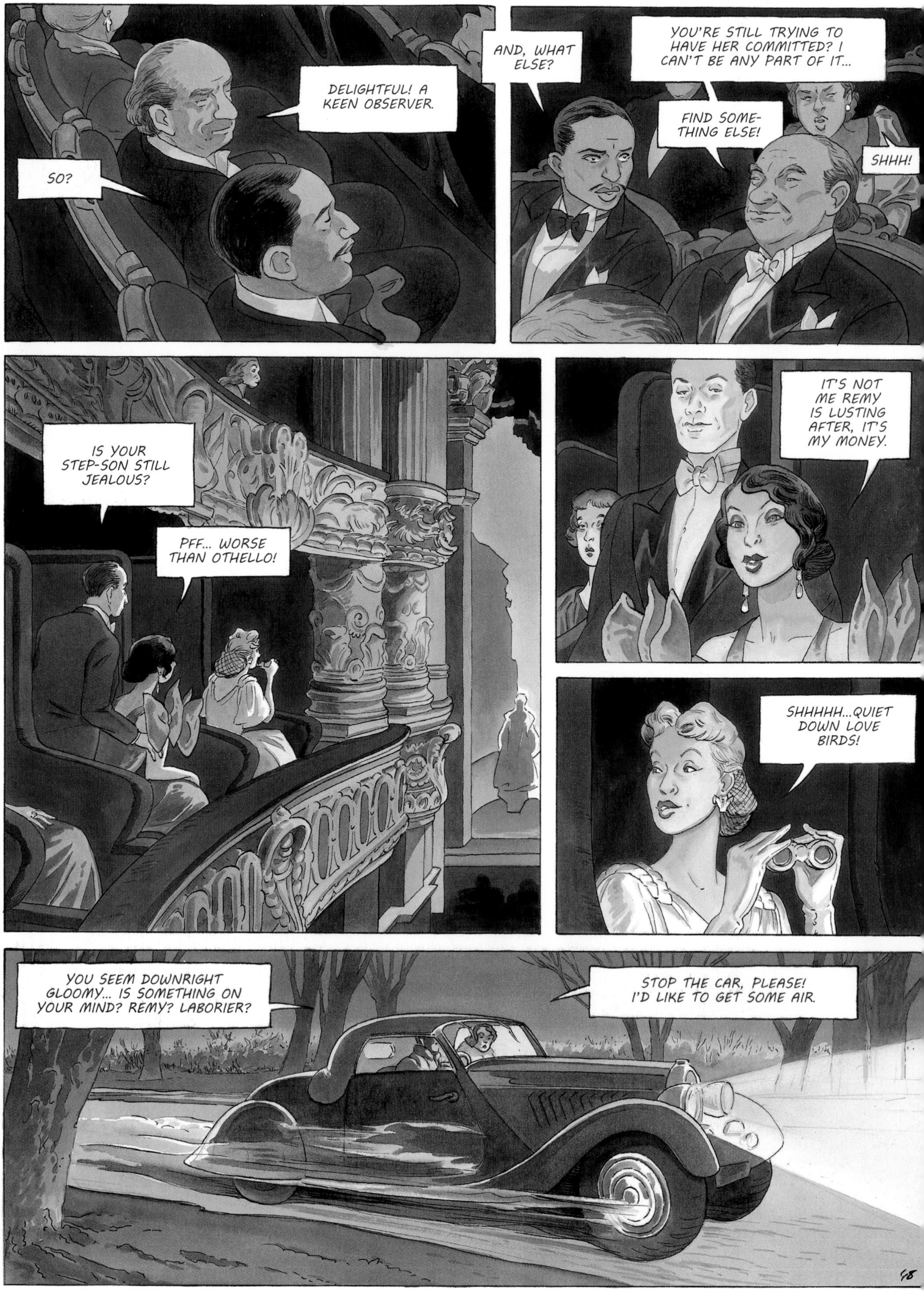
DELIGHTFUL! A KEEN OBSERVER.
SO?
AND, WHAT ELSE?
YOU'RE STILL TRYING TO HAVE HER COMMITTED? I CAN'T BE ANY PART OF IT...
FIND SOMETHING ELSE!
SHHH!
IS YOUR STEP-SON STILL JEALOUS?
PFF... WORSE THAN OTHELLO!
IT'S NOT ME REMY IS LUSTING AFTER, IT'S MY MONEY.
SHHHHH...QUIET DOWN LOVE BIRDS!
YOU SEEM DOWNRIGHT GLOOMY... IS SOMETHING ON YOUR MIND? REMY? LABORIER?
STOP THE CAR, PLEASE! I'D LIKE TO GET SOME AIR.

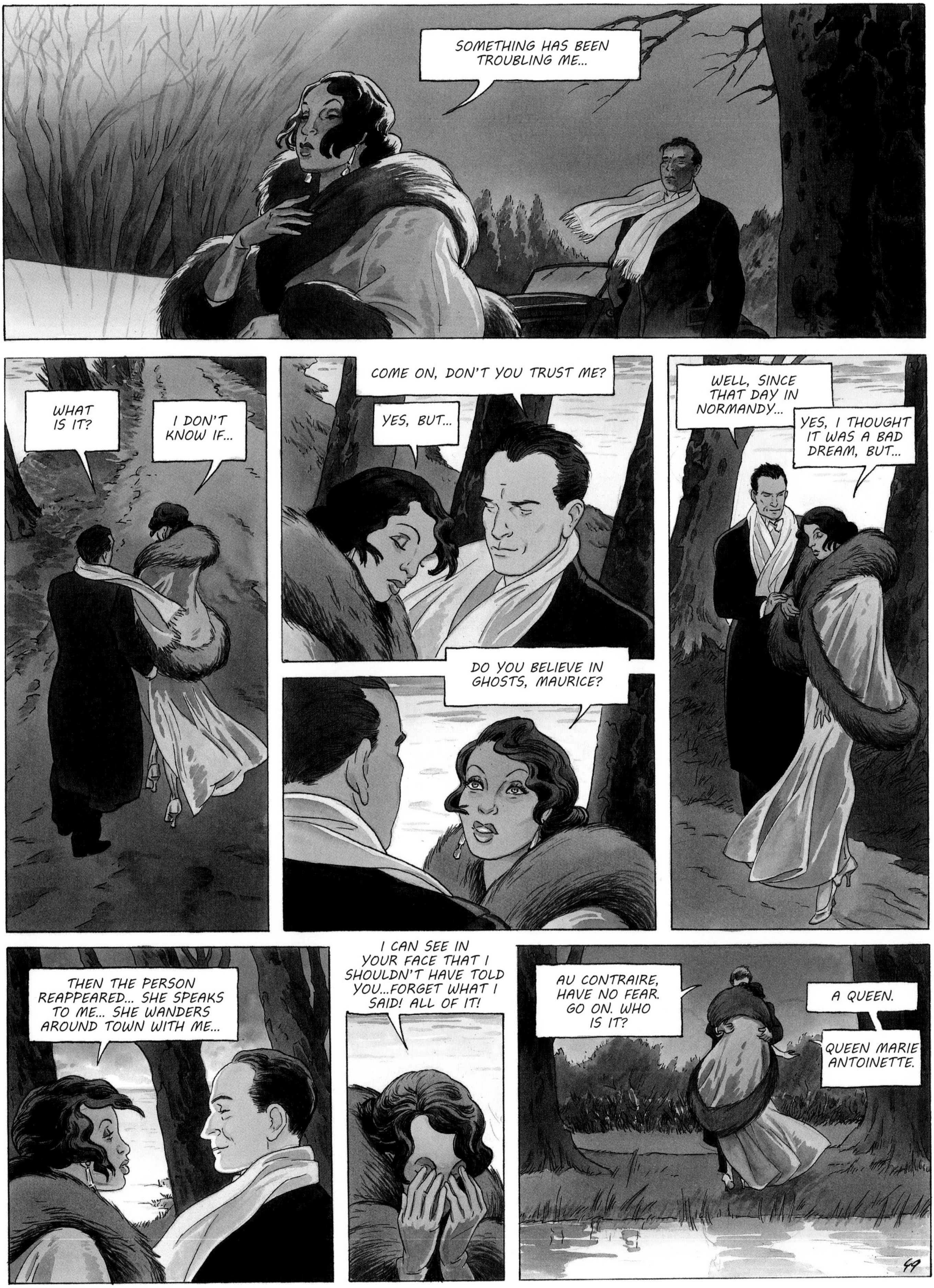
SOMETHING HAS BEEN TROUBLING ME...
WHAT IS IT?
I DON'T KNOW IF...
COME ON, DON'T YOU TRUST ME?
YES, BUT...
DO YOU BELIEVE IN GHOSTS, MAURICE?
WELL, SINCE THAT DAY IN NORMANDY...
YES, I THOUGHT IT WAS A BAD DREAM, BUT...
THEN THE PERSON REAPPEARED... SHE SPEAKS TO ME... SHE WANDERS AROUND TOWN WITH ME...
I CAN SEE IN YOUR FACE THAT I SHOULDN'T HAVE TOLD YOU...FORGET WHAT I SAID! ALL OF IT!
AU CONTRAIRE, HAVE NO FEAR. GO ON. WHO IS IT?
A QUEEN.
QUEEN MARIE ANTOINETTE.
49

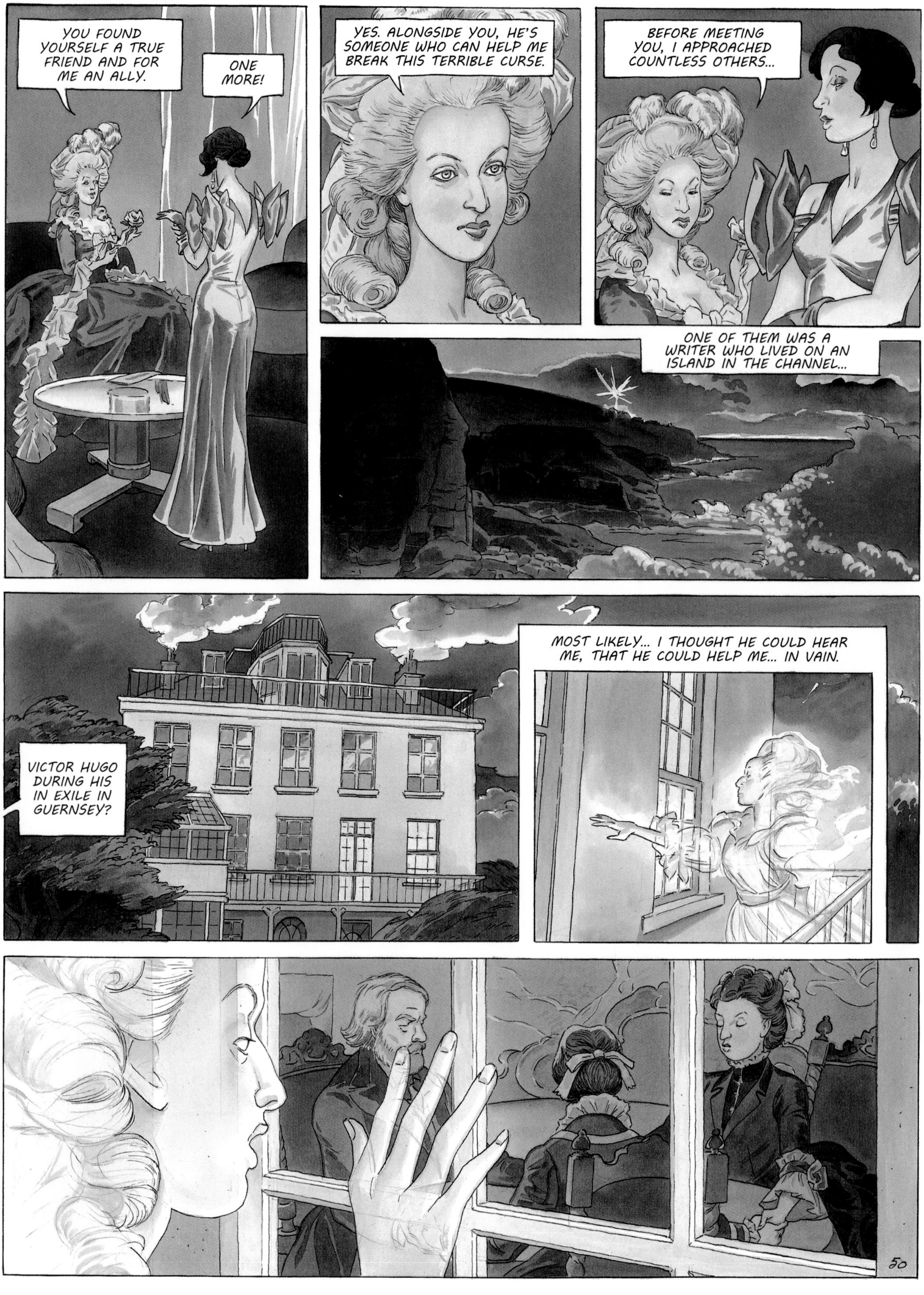
YOU FOUND YOURSELF A TRUE FRIEND AND FOR ME AN ALLY.
ONE MORE!
YES. ALONGSIDE YOU, HE'S SOMEONE WHO CAN HELP ME BREAK THIS TERRIBLE CURSE.
BEFORE MEETING YOU, I APPROACHED COUNTLESS OTHERS...
ONE OF THEM WAS A WRITER WHO LIVED ON AN ISLAND IN THE CHANNEL...
VICTOR HUGO DURING HIS IN EXILE IN GUERNSEY?
MOST LIKELY... I THOUGHT HE COULD HEAR ME, THAT HE COULD HELP ME... IN VAIN.
50

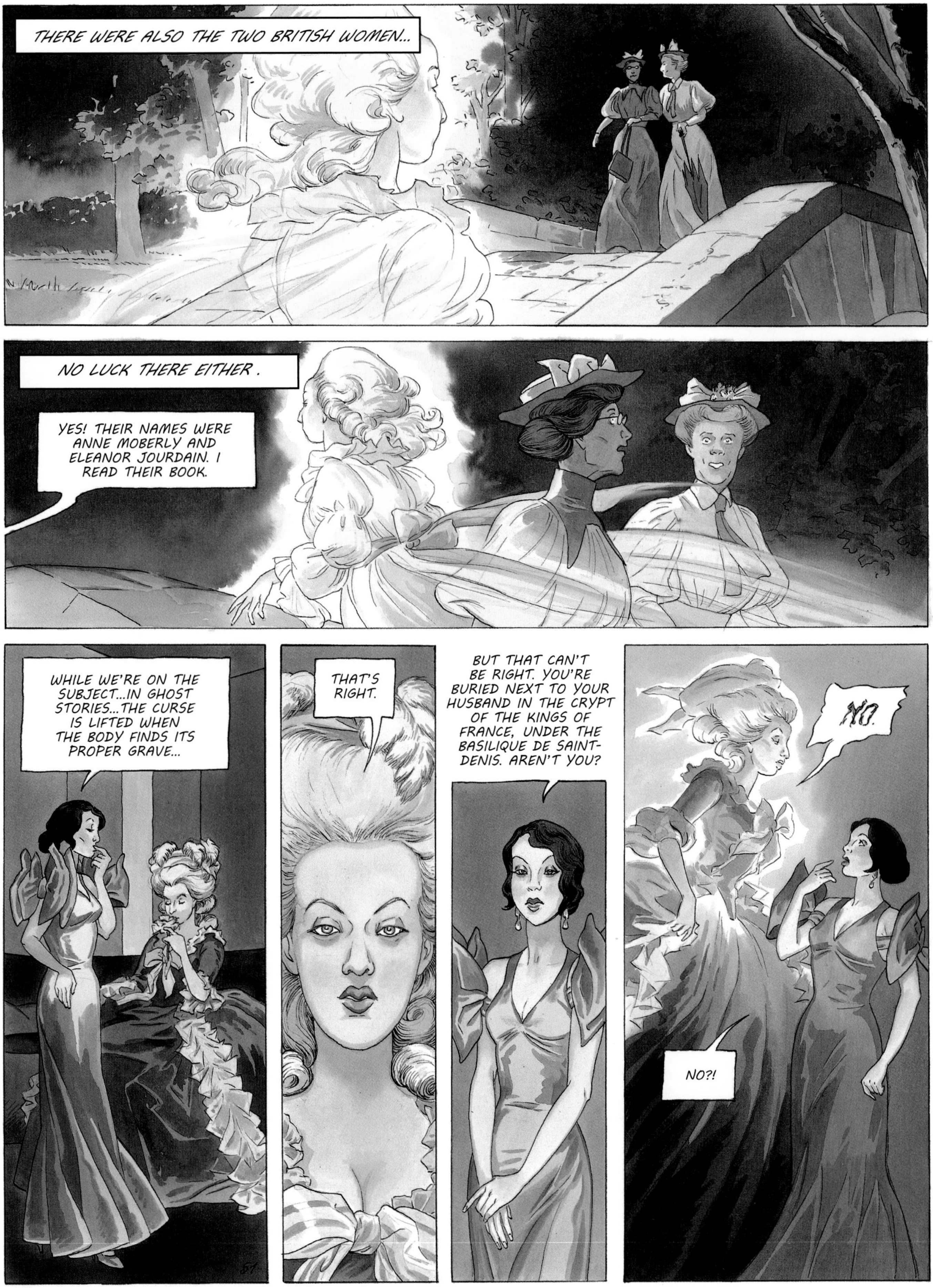
THERE WERE ALSO THE TWO BRITISH WOMEN...
NO LUCK THERE EITHER .
YES! THEIR NAMES WERE ANNE MOBERLY AND ELEANOR JOURDAIN. I READ THEIR BOOK.
WHILE WE'RE ON THE SUBJECT...IN GHOST STORIES...THE CURSE IS LIFTED WHEN THE BODY FINDS ITS PROPER GRAVE...
THAT'S RIGHT.
BUT THAT CAN'T BE RIGHT. YOU'RE BURIED NEXT TO YOUR HUSBAND IN THE CRYPT OF THE KINGS OF FRANCE, UNDER THE BASILIQUE DE SAINT-DENIS. AREN'T YOU?
NO.
NO?!

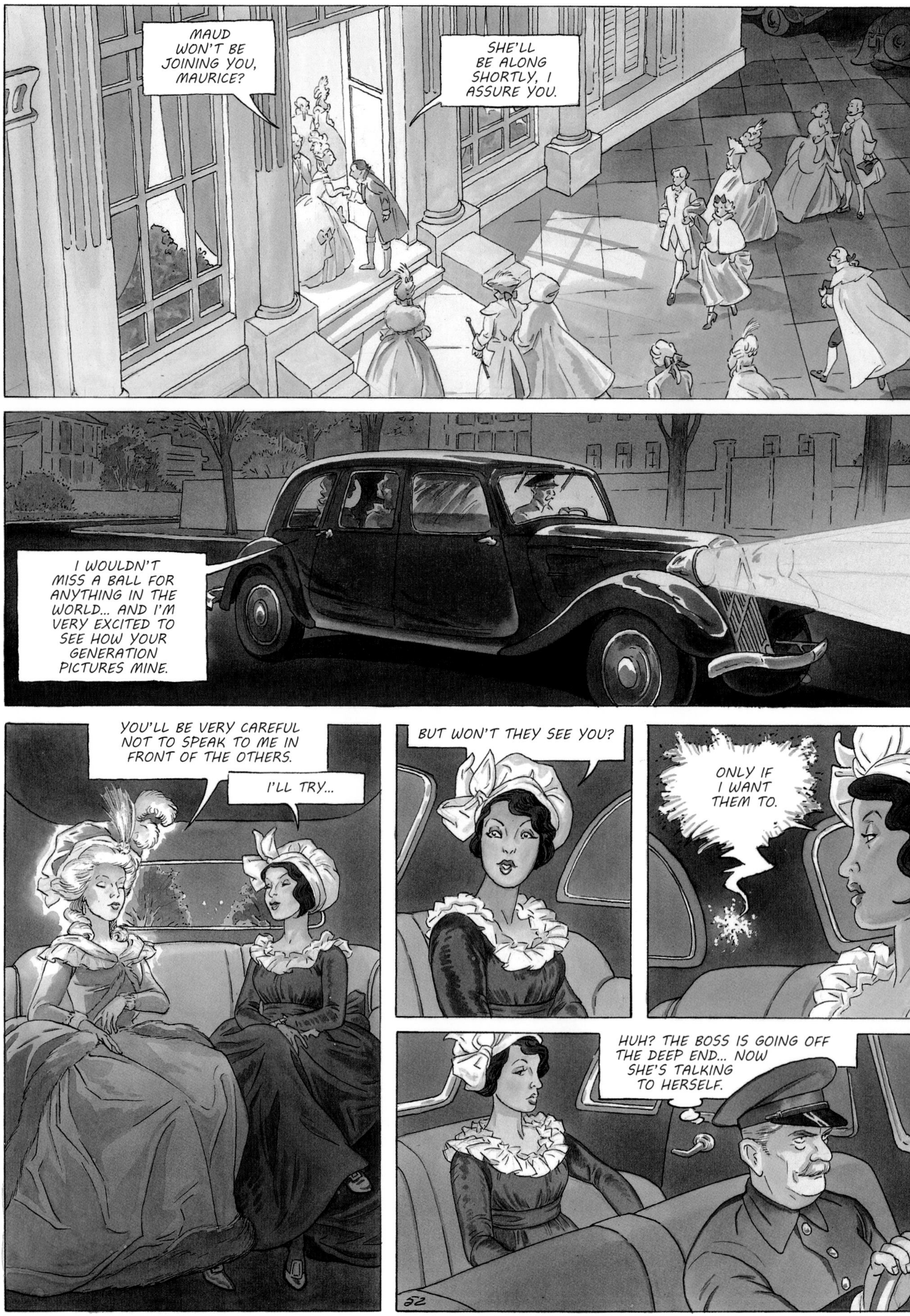
MAUD WON'T BE JOINING YOU, MAURICE?
SHE'LL BE ALONG SHORTLY, I ASSURE YOU.
I WOULDN'T MISS A BALL FOR ANYTHING IN THE WORLD... AND I'M VERY EXCITED TO SEE HOW YOUR GENERATION PICTURES MINE.
YOU'LL BE VERY CAREFUL NOT TO SPEAK TO ME IN FRONT OF THE OTHERS.
I'LL TRY...
BUT WON'T THEY SEE YOU?
ONLY IF I WANT THEM TO.
HUH? THE BOSS IS GOING OFF THE DEEP END... NOW SHE'S TALKING TO HERSELF.

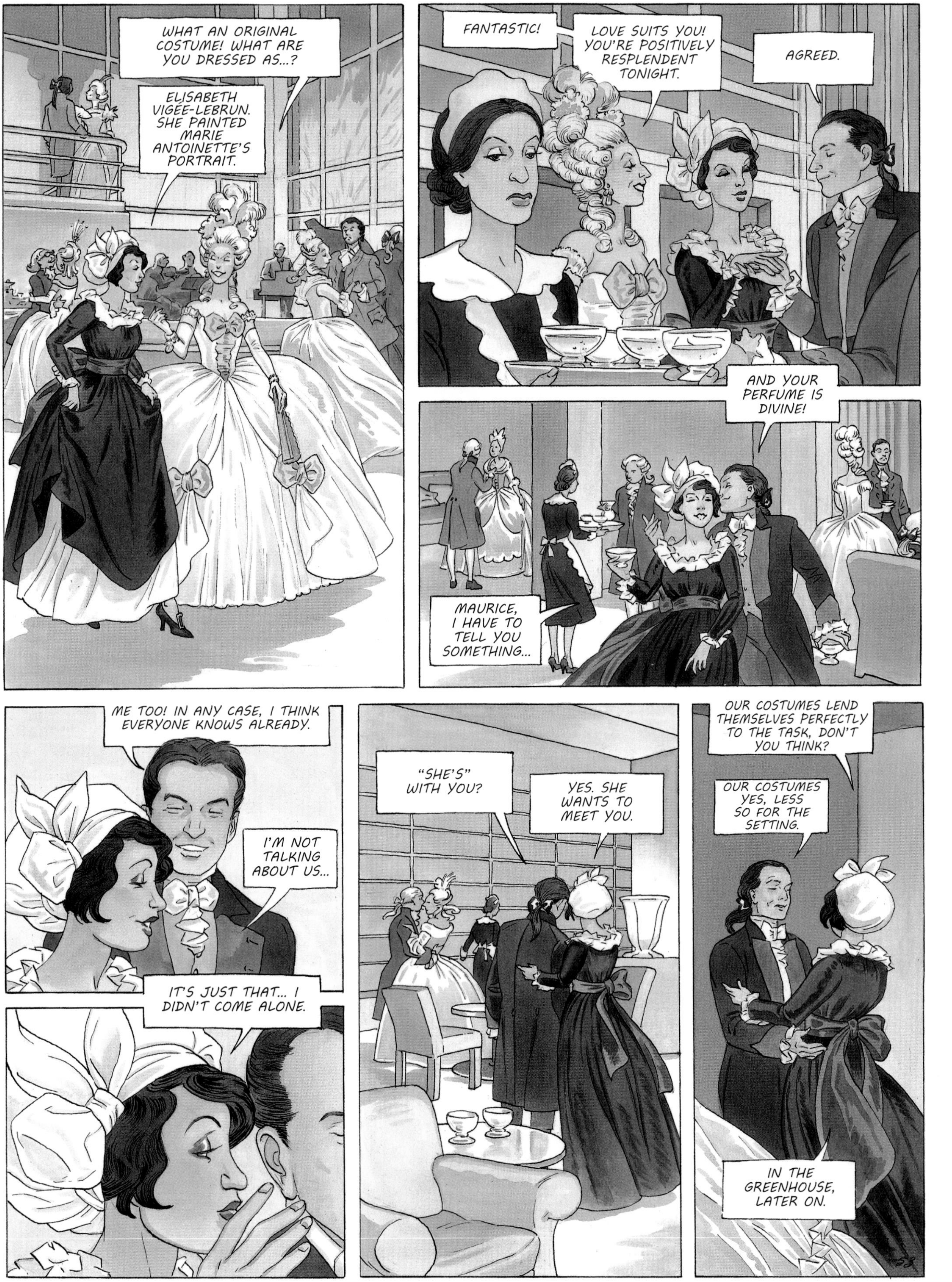
WHAT AN ORIGINAL COSTUME! WHAT ARE YOU DRESSED AS...?
ELISABETH VIGÉE-LEBRUN. SHE PAINTED MARIE ANTOINETTE'S PORTRAIT.
FANTASTIC!
LOVE SUITS YOU! YOU'RE POSITIVELY RESPLENDENT TONIGHT.
AGREED.
AND YOUR PERFUME IS DIVINE!
MAURICE, I HAVE TO TELL YOU SOMETHING...
ME TOO! IN ANY CASE, I THINK EVERYONE KNOWS ALREADY.
I'M NOT TALKING ABOUT US...
IT'S JUST THAT... I DIDN'T COME ALONE.
"SHE'S" WITH YOU?
YES. SHE WANTS TO MEET YOU.
OUR COSTUMES LEND THEMSELVES PERFECTLY TO THE TASK, DON'T YOU THINK?
OUR COSTUMES YES, LESS SO FOR THE SETTING.
IN THE GREENHOUSE, LATER ON.

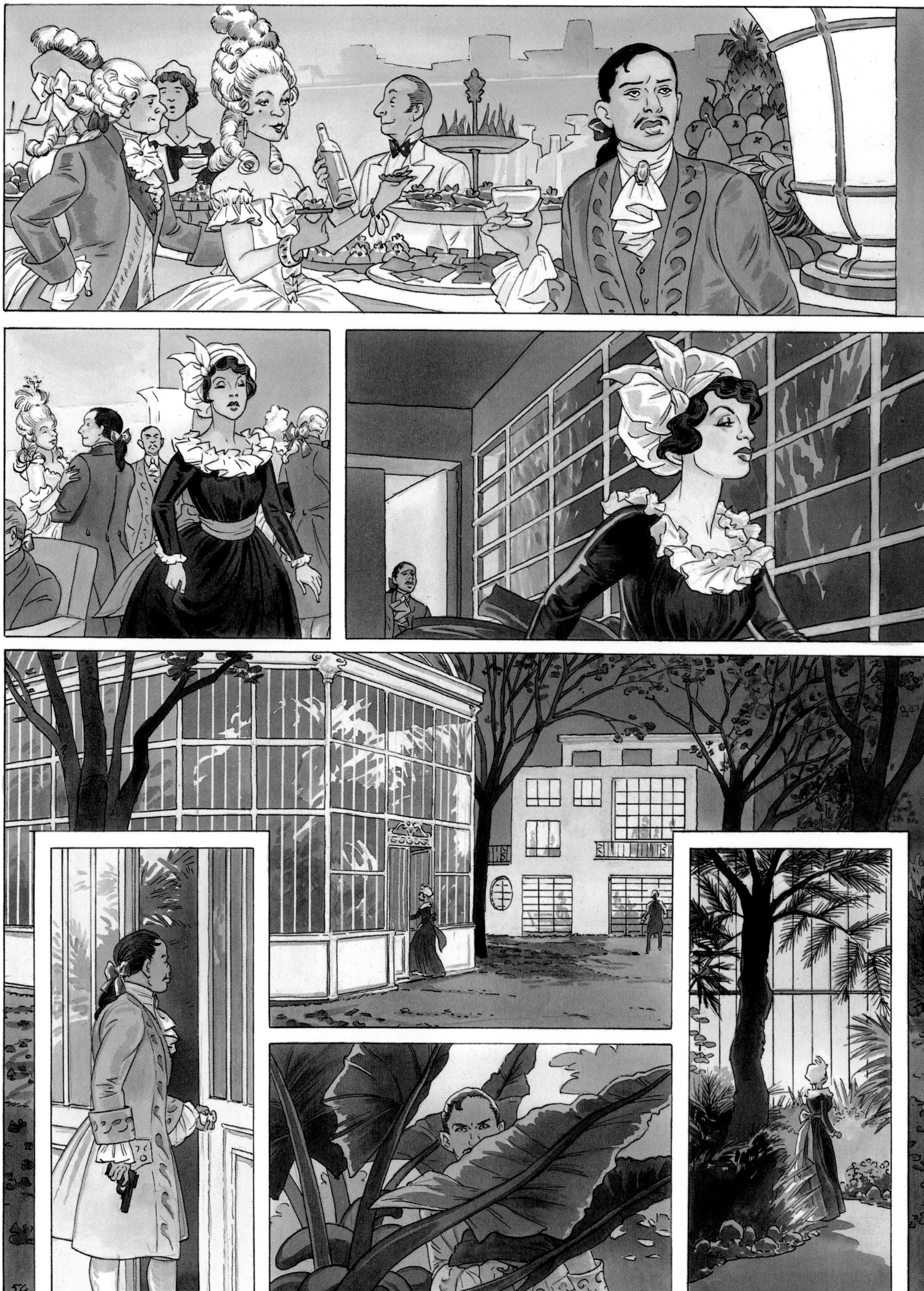

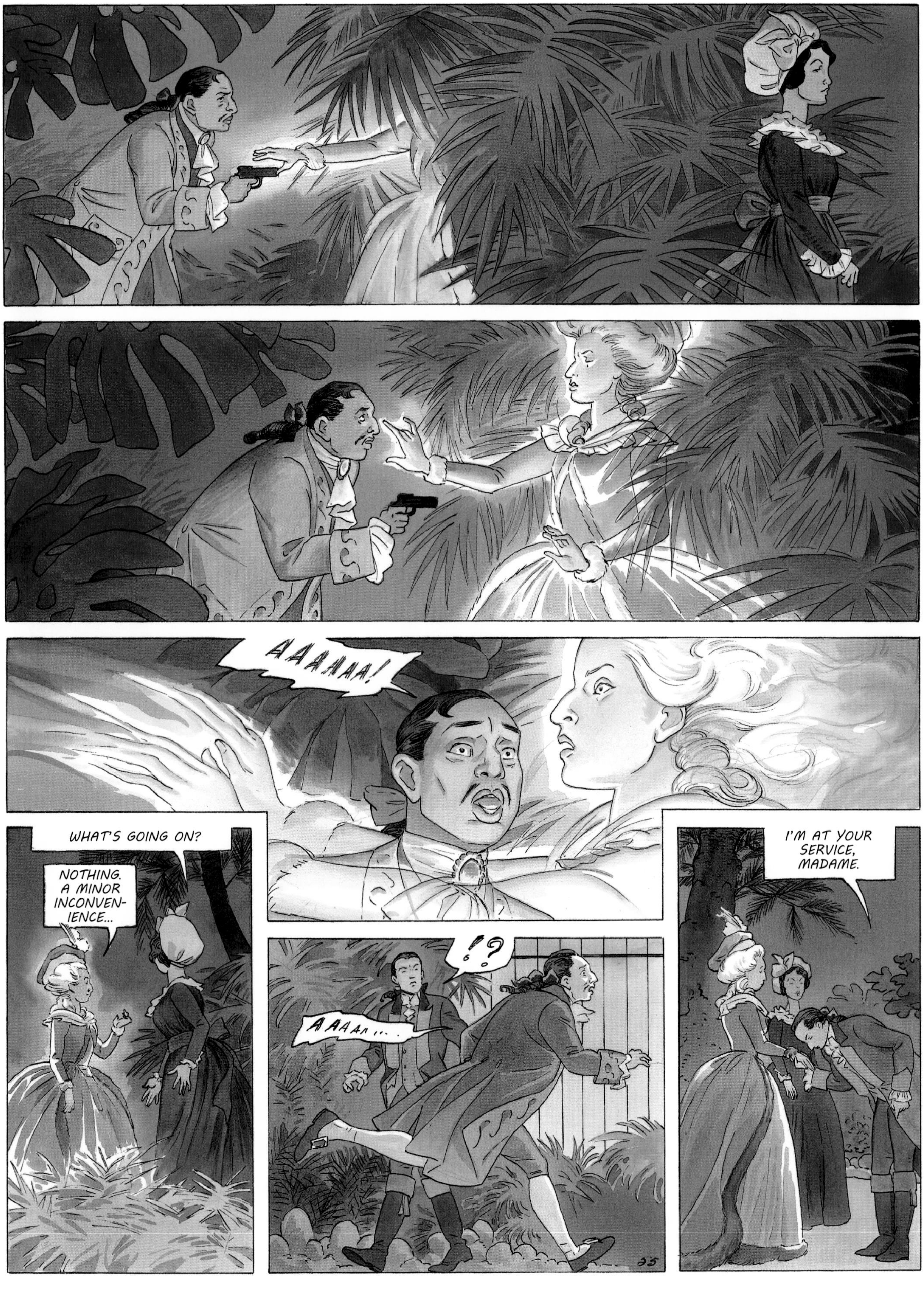
AAAAAA!
WHAT'S GOING ON?
NOTHING. A MINOR INCONVENIENCE...
!?
AAAA...
I'M AT YOUR SERVICE, MADAME.

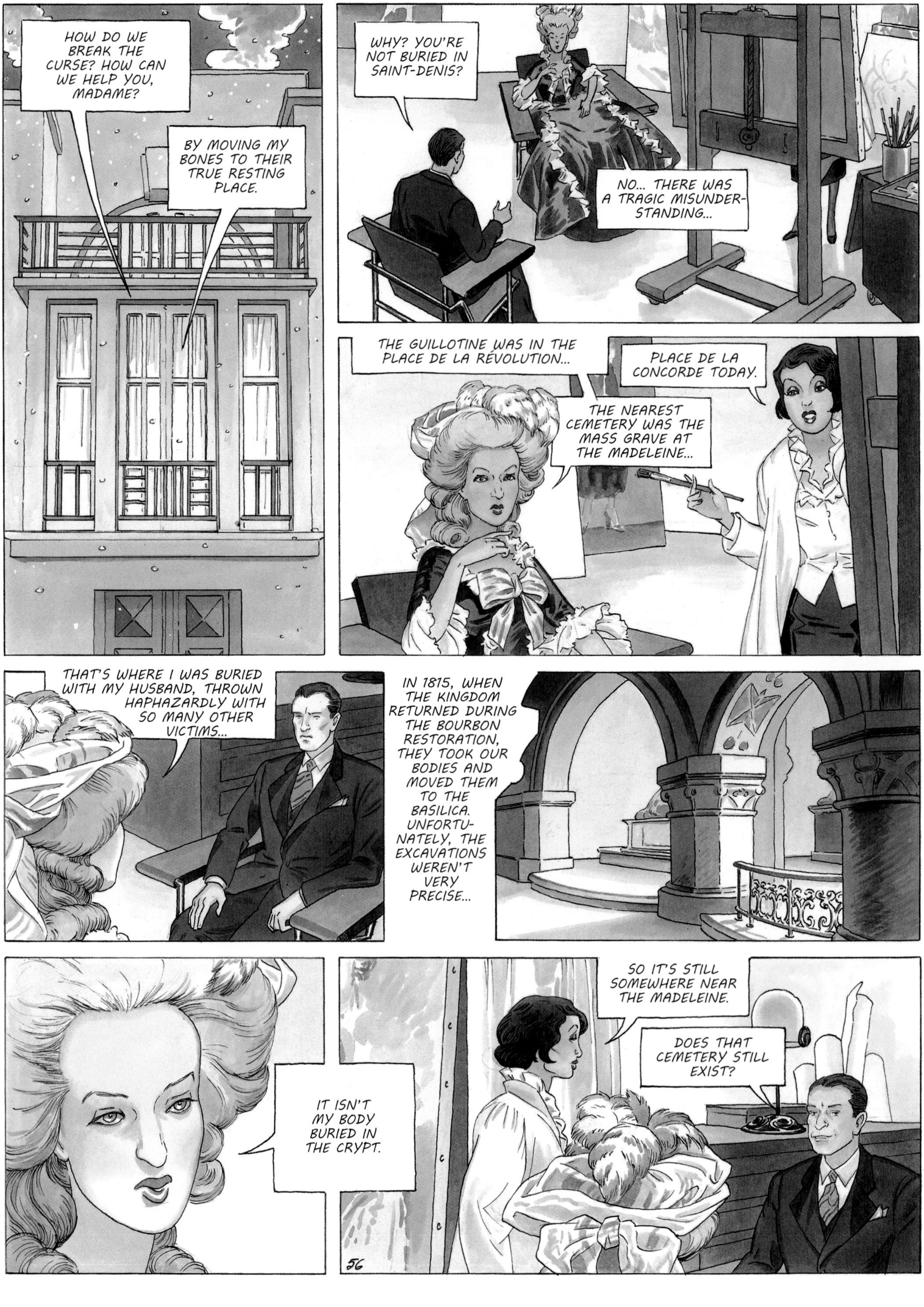
HOW DO WE BREAK THE CURSE? HOW CAN WE HELP YOU, MADAME?
BY MOVING MY BONES TO THEIR TRUE RESTING PLACE.
WHY? YOU'RE NOT BURIED IN SAINT-DENIS?
NO... THERE WAS A TRAGIC MISUNDER-STANDING...
THE GUILLOTINE WAS IN THE PLACE DE LA RÉVOLUTION...
PLACE DE LA CONCORDE TODAY.
THE NEAREST CEMETERY WAS THE MASS GRAVE AT THE MADELEINE...
THAT'S WHERE I WAS BURIED WITH MY HUSBAND, THROWN HAPHAZARDLY WITH SO MANY OTHER VICTIMS...
IN 1815, WHEN THE KINGDOM RETURNED DURING THE BOURBON RESTORATION, THEY TOOK OUR BODIES AND MOVED THEM TO THE BASILICA. UNFORTU-NATELY, THE EXCAVATIONS WEREN'T VERY PRECISE...
IT ISN'T MY BODY BURIED IN THE CRYPT.
SO IT'S STILL SOMEWHERE NEAR THE MADELEINE.
DOES THAT CEMETERY STILL EXIST?
56

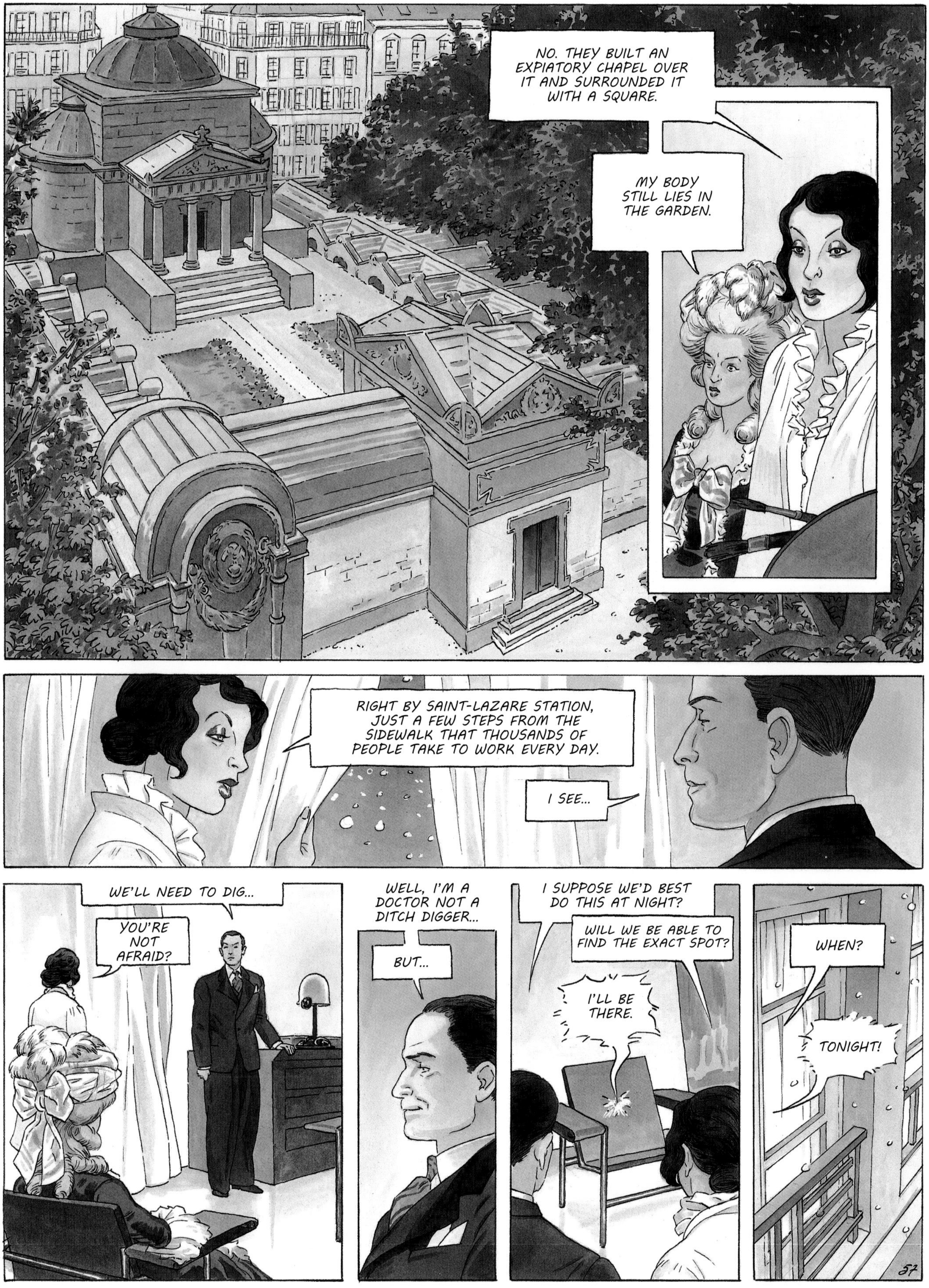
NO. THEY BUILT AN EXPIATORY CHAPEL OVER IT AND SURROUNDED IT WITH A SQUARE.
MY BODY STILL LIES IN THE GARDEN.
RIGHT BY SAINT-LAZARE STATION, JUST A FEW STEPS FROM THE SIDEWALK THAT THOUSANDS OF PEOPLE TAKE TO WORK EVERY DAY.
I SEE...
WE'LL NEED TO DIG...
YOU'RE NOT AFRAID?
WELL, I'M A DOCTOR NOT A DITCH DIGGER...
BUT...
I SUPPOSE WE'D BEST DO THIS AT NIGHT?
WILL WE BE ABLE TO FIND THE EXACT SPOT?
I'LL BE THERE.
WHEN?
TONIGHT!
57

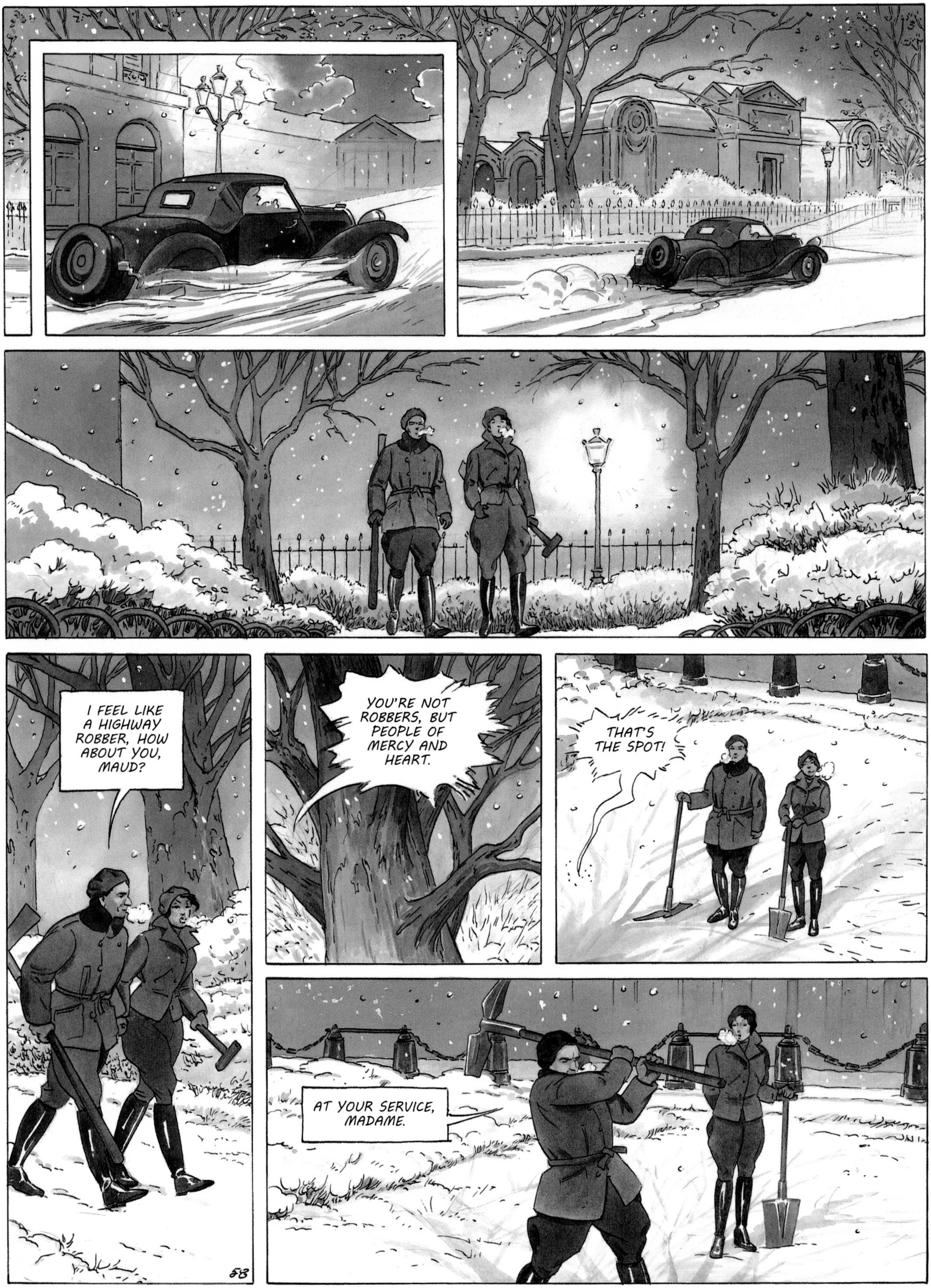
I FEEL LIKE A HIGHWAY ROBBER, HOW ABOUT YOU, MAUD?
YOU'RE NOT ROBBERS, BUT PEOPLE OF MERCY AND HEART.
THAT'S THE SPOT!
AT YOUR SERVICE, MADAME.
58

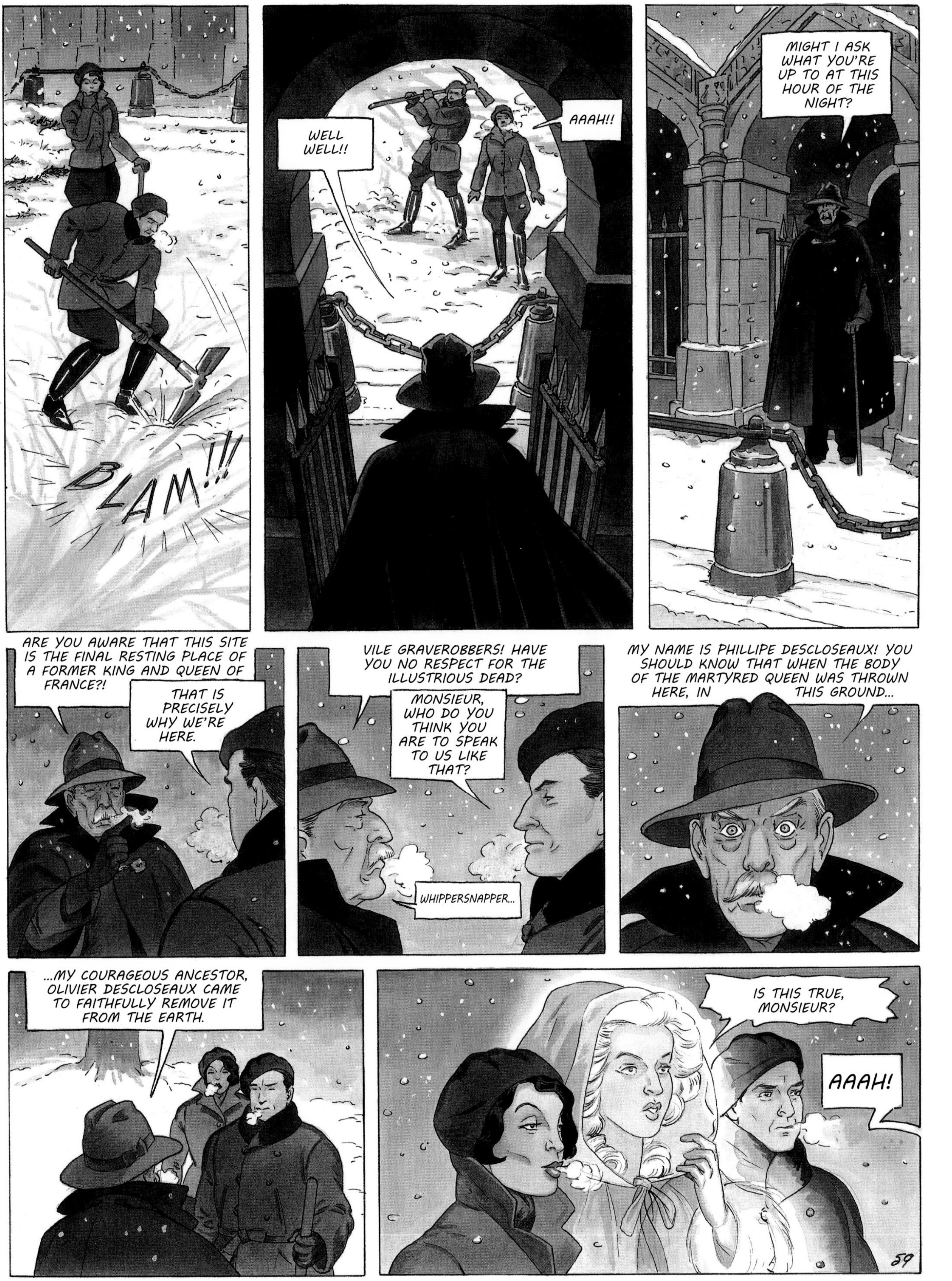
BLAM!!!
WELL WELL!!
AAAH!!
MIGHT I ASK WHAT YOU'RE UP TO AT THIS HOUR OF THE NIGHT?
ARE YOU AWARE THAT THIS SITE IS THE FINAL RESTING PLACE OF A FORMER KING AND QUEEN OF FRANCE?!
THAT IS PRECISELY WHY WE'RE HERE.
VILE GRAVEROBBERS! HAVE YOU NO RESPECT FOR THE ILLUSTRIOUS DEAD?
MONSIEUR, WHO DO YOU THINK YOU ARE TO SPEAK TO US LIKE THAT?
WHIPPERSNAPPER...
MY NAME IS PHILLIPE DESCLOSEAUX! YOU SHOULD KNOW THAT WHEN THE BODY OF THE MARTYRED QUEEN WAS THROWN HERE, IN THIS GROUND...
...MY COURAGEOUS ANCESTOR, OLIVIER DESCLOSEAUX CAME TO FAITHFULLY REMOVE IT FROM THE EARTH.
IS THIS TRUE, MONSIEUR?
AAAH!
59

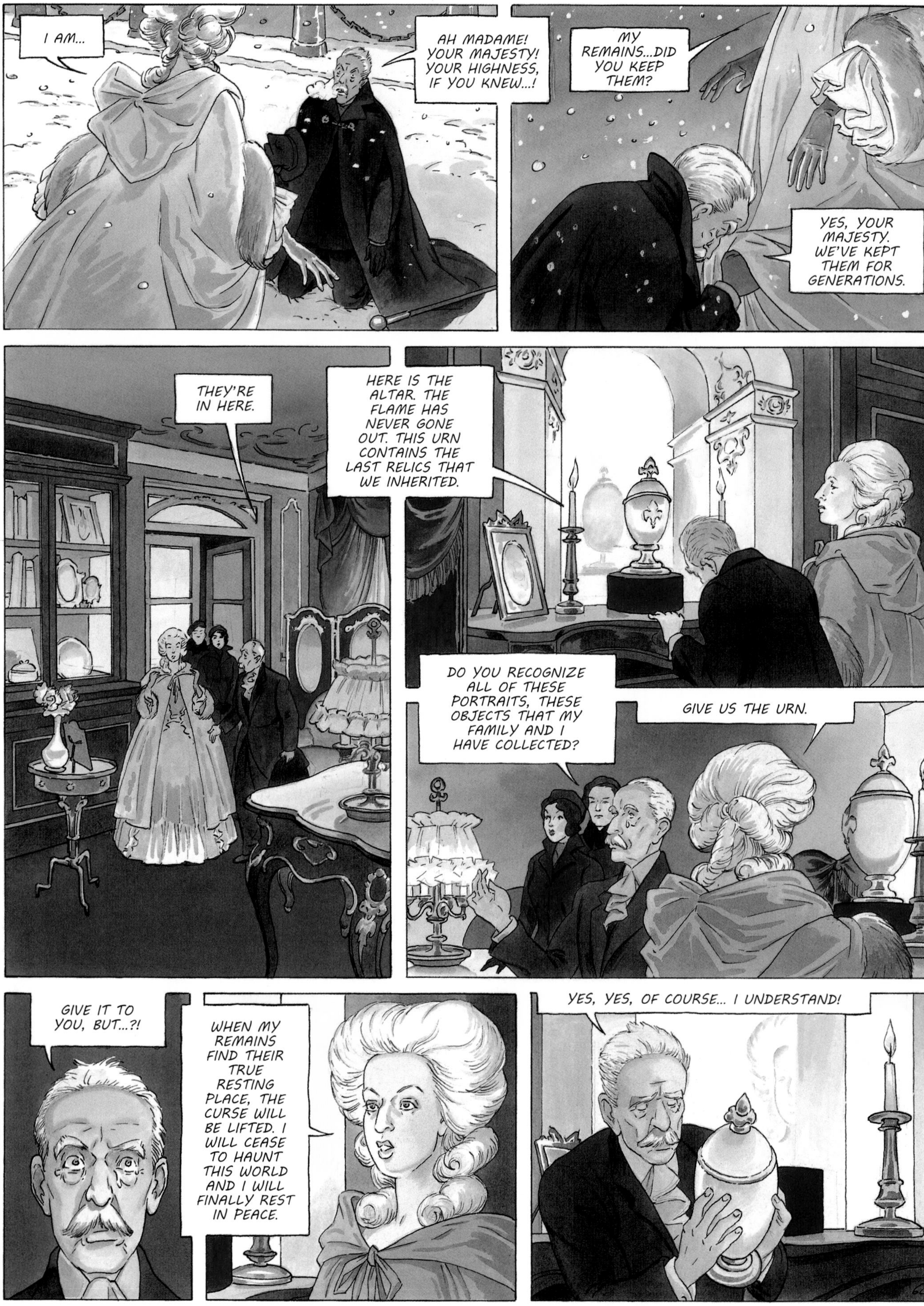
I AM...
AH MADAME! YOUR MAJESTY! YOUR HIGHNESS, IF YOU KNEW...!
MY REMAINS...DID YOU KEEP THEM?
YES, YOUR MAJESTY. WE'VE KEPT THEM FOR GENERATIONS.
THEY'RE IN HERE.
HERE IS THE ALTAR. THE FLAME HAS NEVER GONE OUT. THIS URN CONTAINS THE LAST RELICS THAT WE INHERITED.
DO YOU RECOGNIZE ALL OF THESE PORTRAITS, THESE OBJECTS THAT MY FAMILY AND I HAVE COLLECTED?
GIVE US THE URN.
GIVE IT TO YOU, BUT...?!
WHEN MY REMAINS FIND THEIR TRUE RESTING PLACE, THE CURSE WILL BE LIFTED. I WILL CEASE TO HAUNT THIS WORLD AND I WILL FINALLY REST IN PEACE.
YES, YES, OF COURSE... I UNDERSTAND!
60

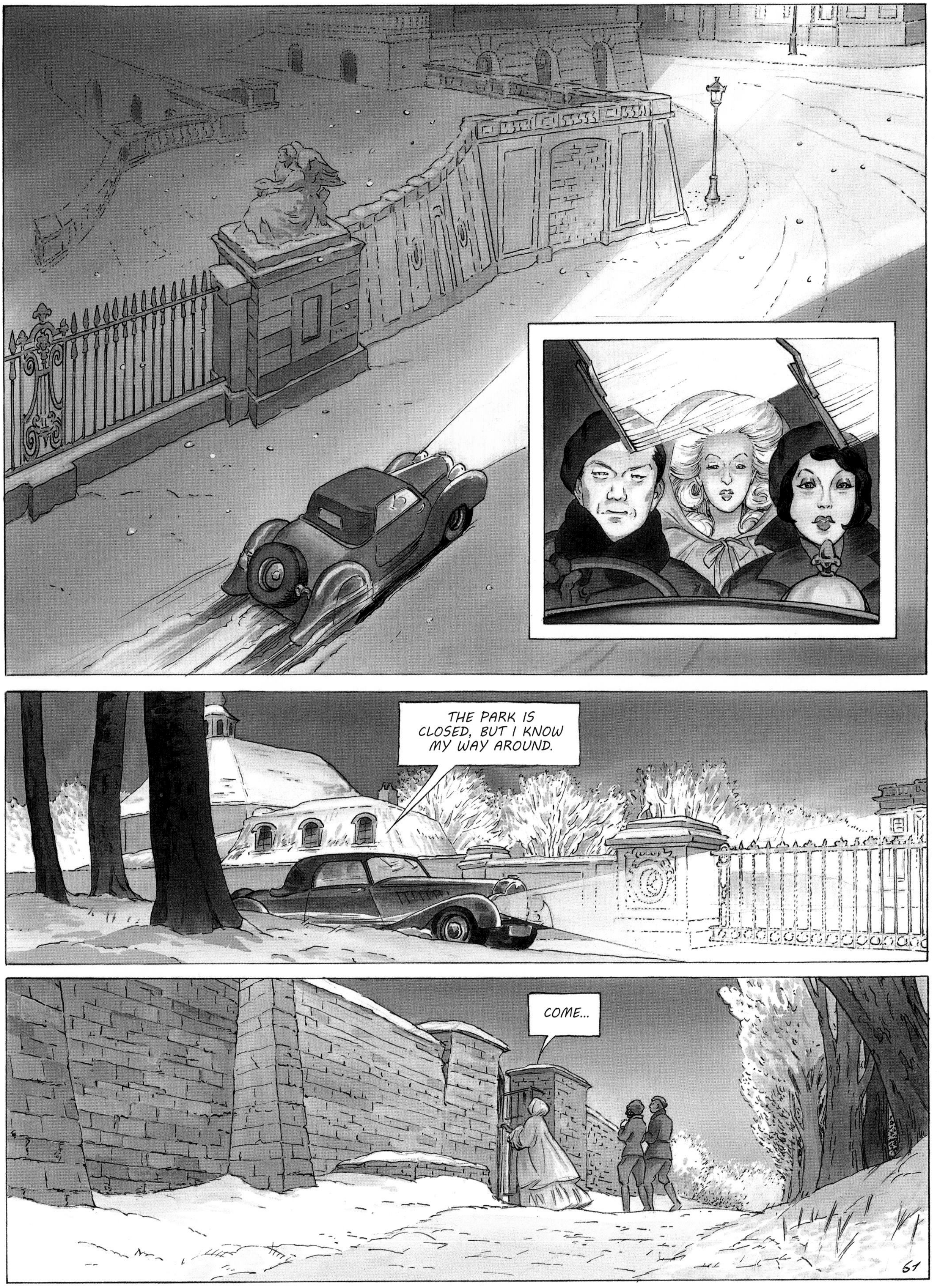
THE PARK IS CLOSED, BUT I KNOW MY WAY AROUND.
COME...
61

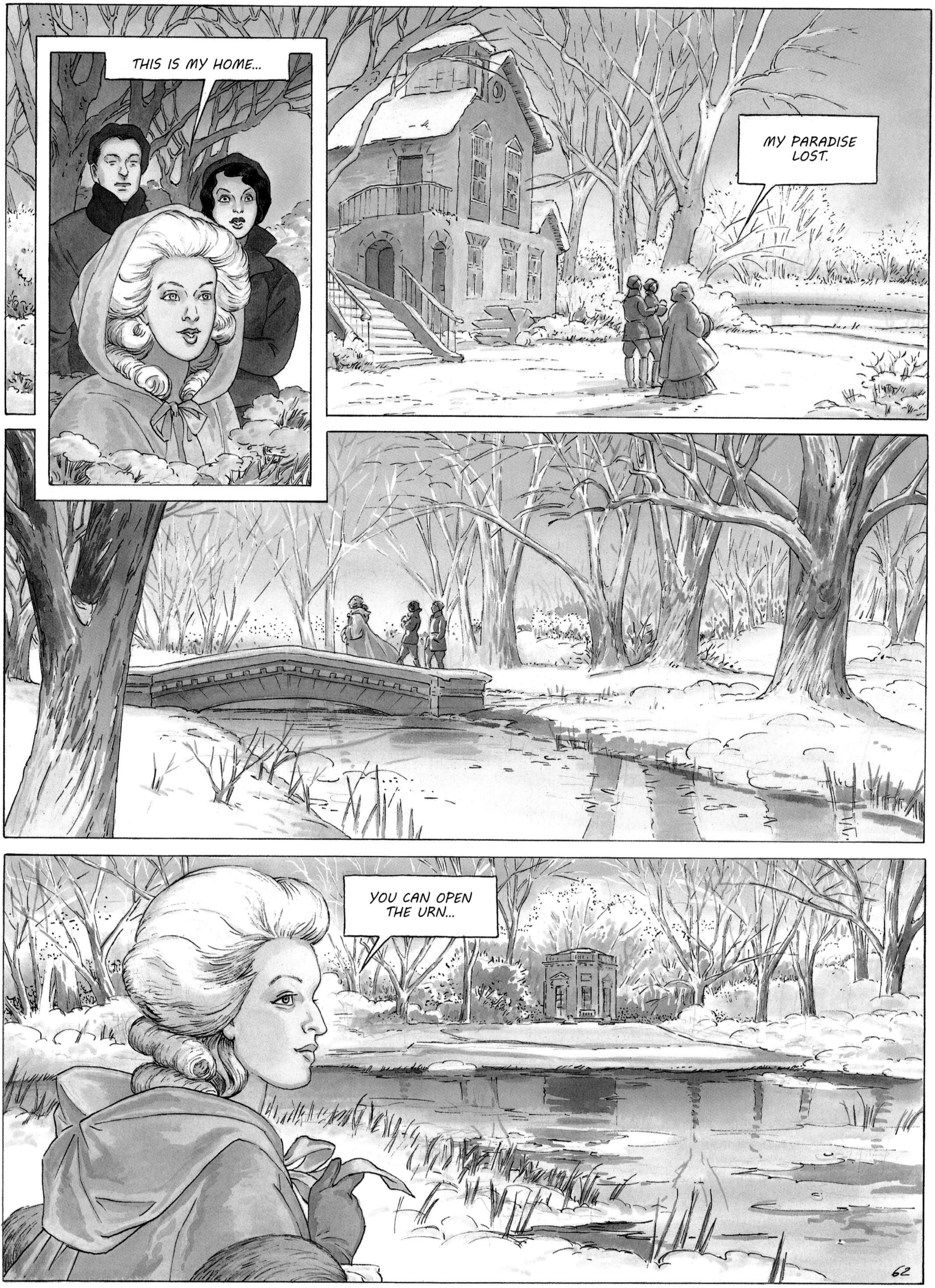
THIS IS MY HOME...
MY PARADISE LOST.
YOU CAN OPEN THE URN...
62

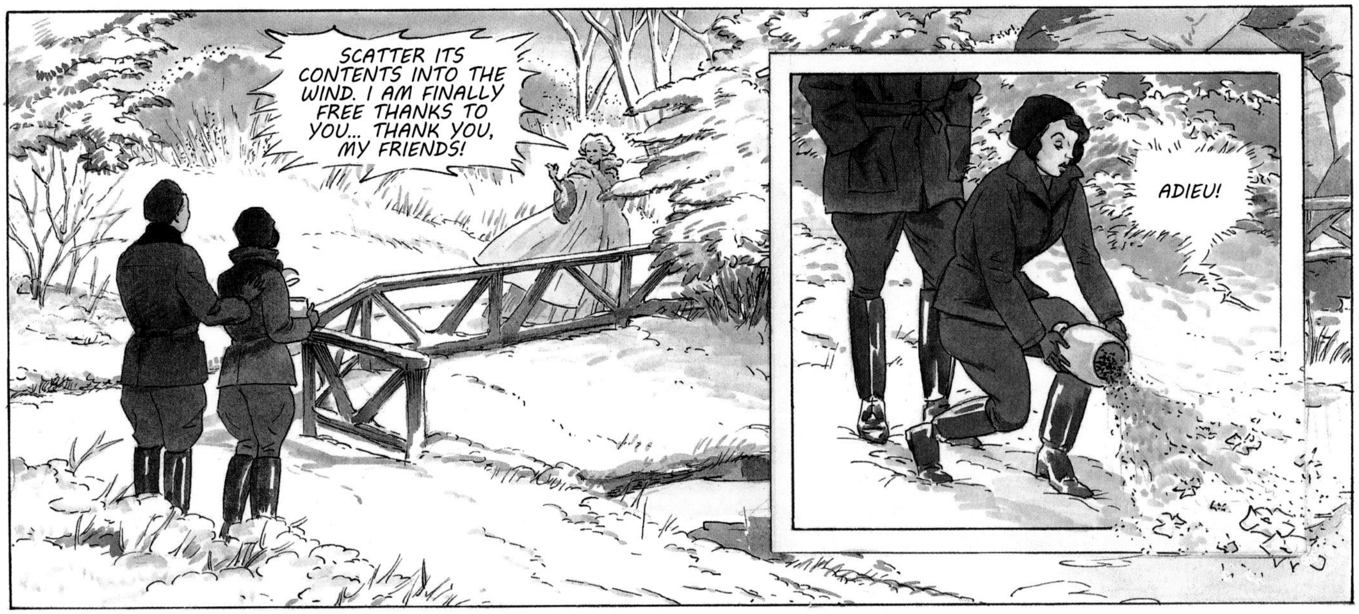
SCATTER ITS CONTENTS INTO THE WIND. I AM FINALLY FREE THANKS TO YOU... THANK YOU, MY FRIENDS!
ADIEU!

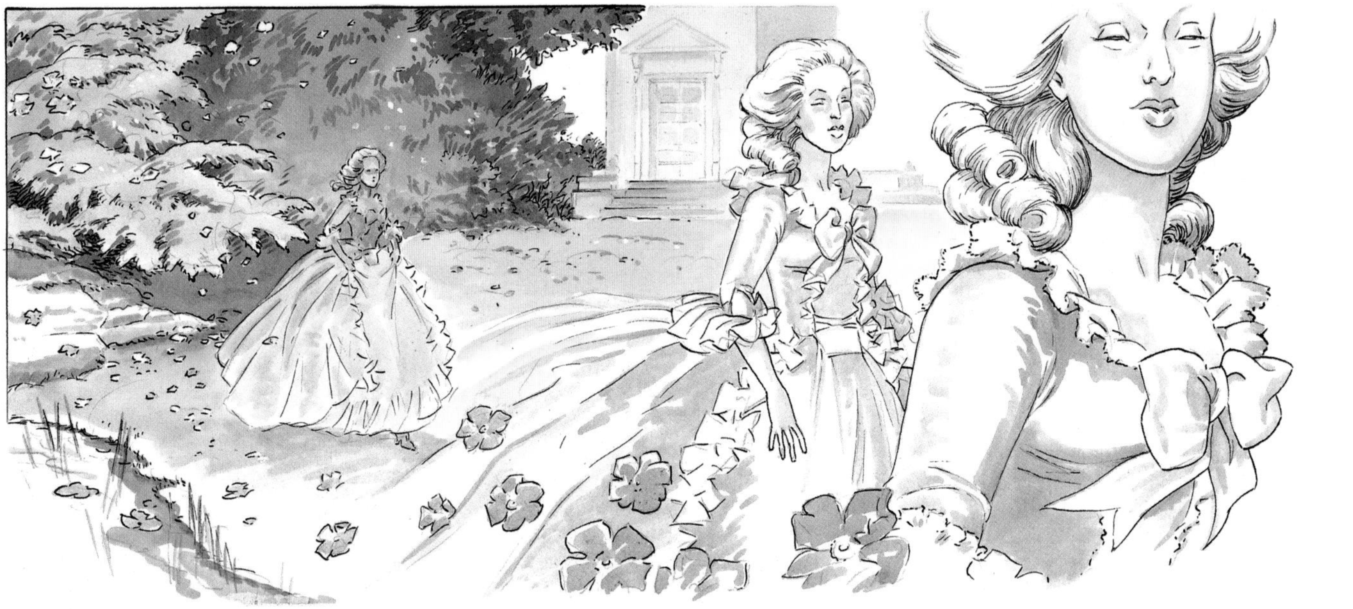

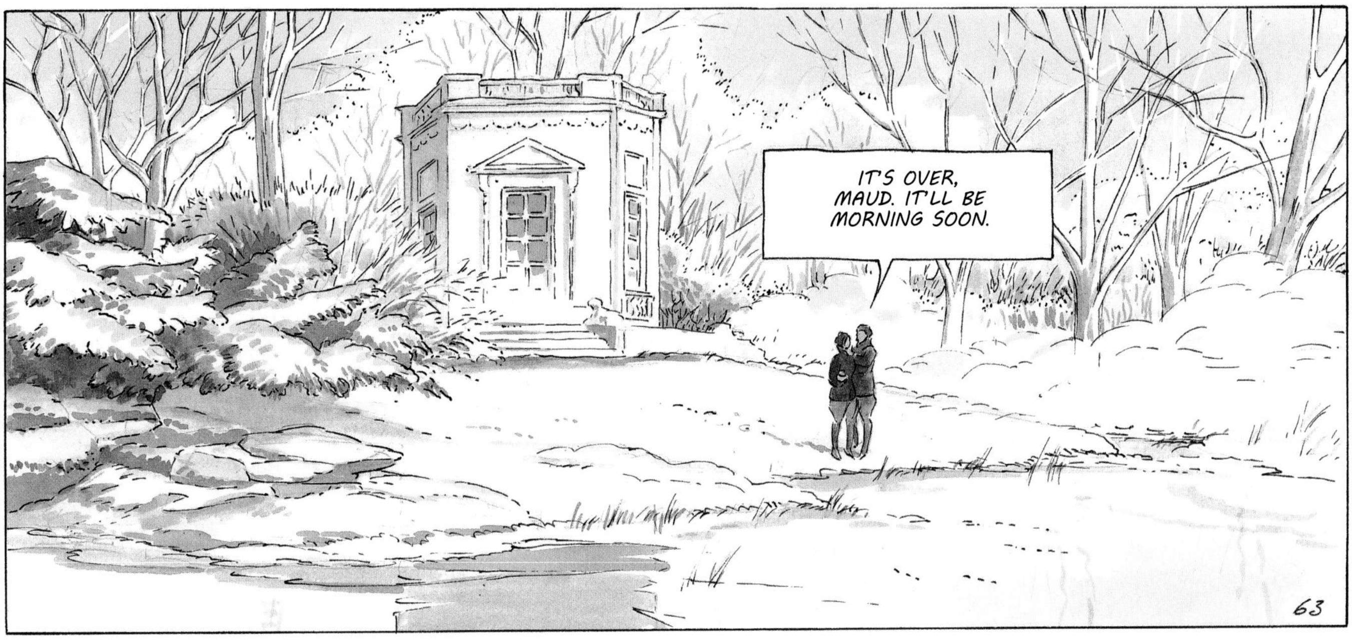
IT'S OVER, MAUD. IT'LL BE MORNING SOON.
63

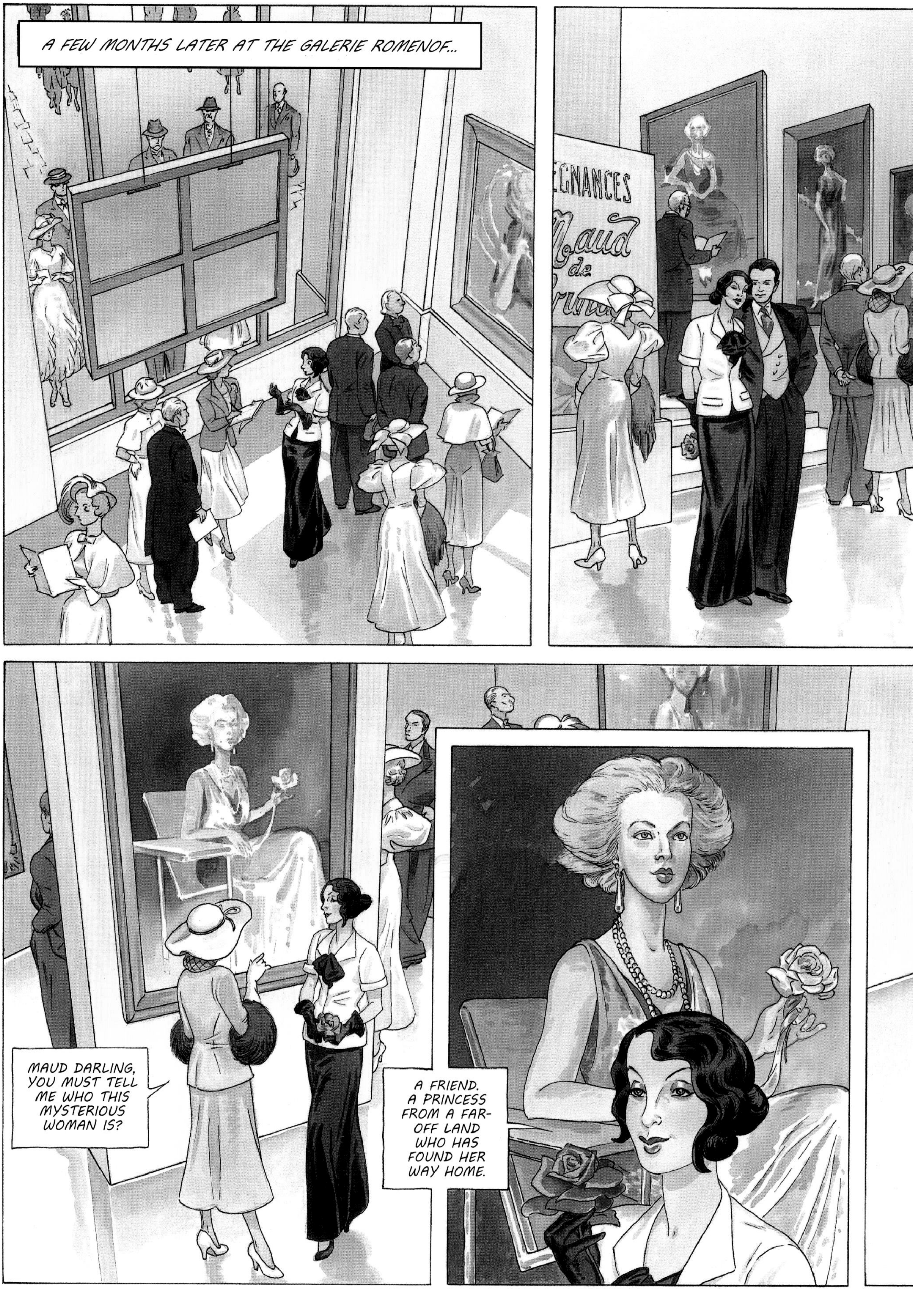
A FEW MONTHS LATER AT THE GALERIE ROMENOF...
EGNANCES
Maud de
MAUD DARLING, YOU MUST TELL ME WHO THIS MYSTERIOUS WOMAN IS?
A FRIEND. A PRINCESS FROM A FAR-OFF LAND WHO HAS FOUND HER WAY HOME.

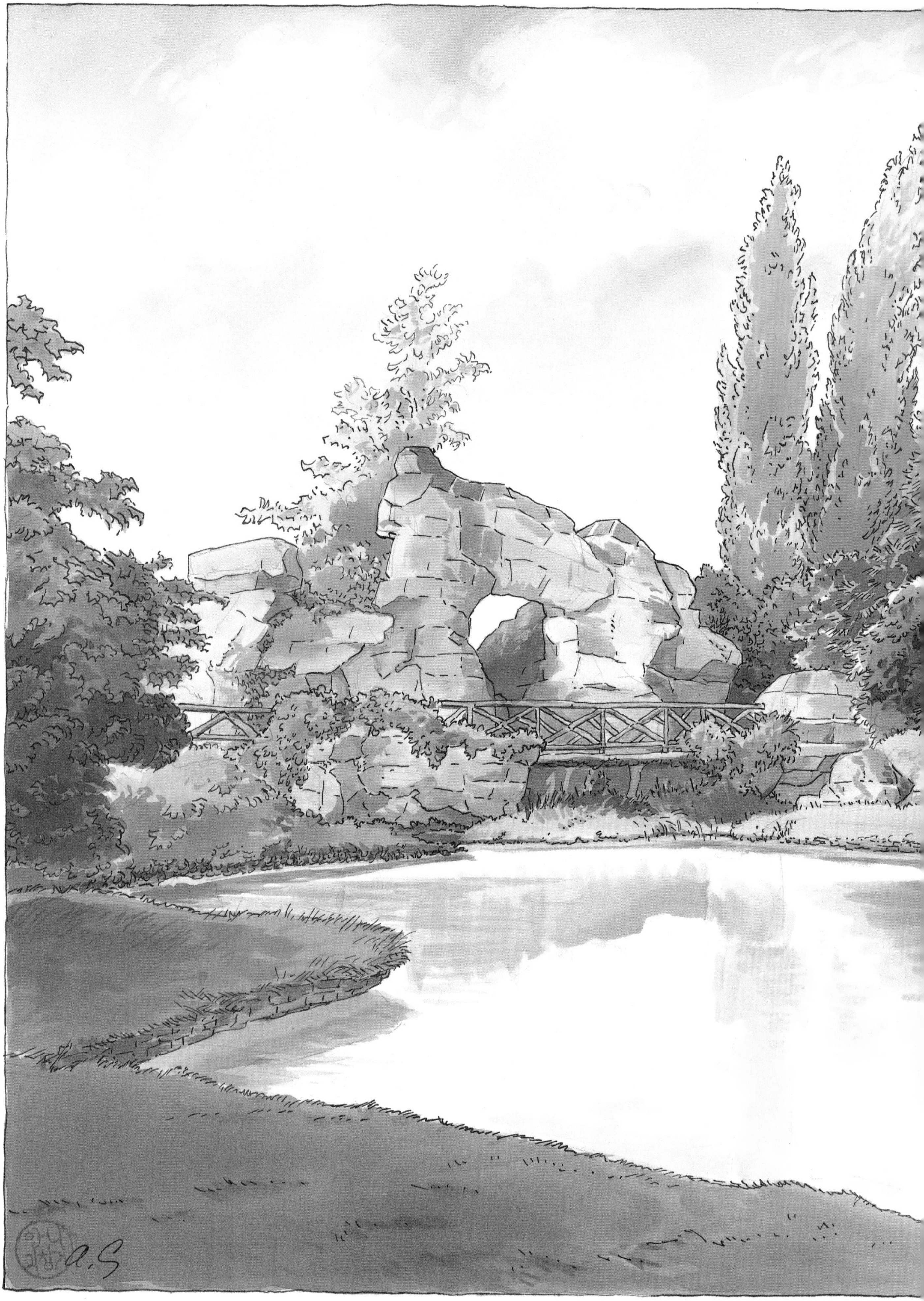